Days of Emotion

Praying with Pope John Paul II
in the Holy Land

Robert F. Keeler and Paul Moses

Resurrection Press
An Imprint of
CATHOLIC BOOK PUBLISHING CO.
Totowa • New Jersey

DEDICATION

To Sister Marnette Bamberger, O.P.,
my beloved first-grade teacher.—Bob Keeler

To Maureen—Paul Moses

First published in March 2001 by
  Catholic Book Publishing/Resurrection Press
  77 West End Road
  Totowa, NJ 07512

Copyright © 2001 by Robert F. Keeler and Paul Moses.

ISBN 1-878718-62-2
Library of Congress Catalog Card Number: 00-135971

Cover design and background photo by John Murello
Inset photo of pope by AP/Wide World Photos
Photos in text by AP/Wide World Photos

Printed in the United States of America

Contents

Acknowledgments

W E thank our editors at *Newsday* for sending us to cover Pope John Paul II's trip to the Holy Land and for guiding us through the coverage. In particular, our thanks go to foreign desk editors Tim Phelps, Michael Muskal and Jack Klein, and to Associate Managing Editor Les Payne. Many thanks also to the Middle East bureau chief for *Newsday*, Matthew McAllester; his researcher, Michal Schonbrun; staff photographer J. Conrad Williams and staff writer Mohamad Bazzi.

We'd like to thank Gunther Lawrence and Ari Goldman for organizing the Religion and Media 2000+ Conference, which helped provide important background for this book. Joseph Cornelius Donnelly of Aid to the Church in Need gave the benefit of his extensive experience in the Middle East, as did Monsignor Robert Stern and Michael LaCivita of Catholic Near East Welfare Association.

Frank DeRosa of the Diocese of Brooklyn's public information office and Jon Kelley and Cedric Chin of the diocese's pastoral communications office, Eric Greenberg, and Father Charles Matonti also provided valuable assistance. We are grateful as well to Charles Lindner, the librarian at the Diocese of Brooklyn's Immaculate Conception Center in Douglaston, and to the monks of Mount Saviour Monastery in Pine City, in upstate New York's Southern Tier, who provided Paul a comfortable and supportive environment to write much of Chapter III.

For her receptiveness to the idea for the book and for her gentle editing touch with the actual text, we owe a debt of gratitude to Emilie Cerar. For their numerous valuable suggestions and careful reading, we extend warm thanks to Cardinal William H. Keeler and Rabbi A. James Rudin.

Finally, and most of all, we thank our families for being patient with us as we hurled ourselves into this labor of love. Paul thanks Maureen, Matthew, and Caitlin, and offers special gratitude to his father, Bernard L. Moses. Bob thanks Judy, Rebekah, Hailey, Rachel and Noel.

Foreword

JEWS and Christians have been making pilgrimages to the land of Israel and Jerusalem for thousands of years. Whether the faithful pilgrims arrived by foot, camel, horse, boat, or jet plane did not matter. What counted was the devotion that each man, woman and child brought to their personal spiritual journey.

Unfortunately, in the past, some Christian pilgrims came as warriors, but most came to the land of the Bible in peace. No pilgrim symbolized peace more than Pope John Paul II, whose mission of faith took place in March 2000.

Among the thousands of media representatives who accompanied the Pope on his pilgrimage were two extraordinary journalists, Robert Keeler and Paul Moses of *Newsday*. Both are world-class reporters with discerning eyes and talented pens. But Keeler and Moses brought something else to Jerusalem as well: two human beings with sensitive hearts and souls who opened themselves to the unique emotions every pilgrim experiences.

The two journalists "covered" the Pope's visit with superb skill. Their daily reports captured the excitement, tension, and drama as John Paul encountered Jews, Christians, and Muslims in the Holy Land. However, Keeler and Moses are also faithful Catholics who allowed themselves to be moved by the people they met and the places they visited. That kind of dual vision is unique and merits praise.

I, too, was privileged to be in Israel during the Pope's historic visit and I can attest to both the professional vigor and religious convictions of Keeler and Moses. I strongly believe this book brilliantly captures those days of "intense emotion."

On a personal note, Keeler and Moses know that I cried with joy when the spiritual leader of the Roman Catholic Church landed at Ben Gurion Airport and was greeted by

Israel's President and Prime Minister. I wept because history had come full circle: the Jewish people were playing host to the world's most celebrated Christian pilgrim.

And happily, Robert Keeler and Paul Moses were there to tell the story.

Rabbi A. James Rudin
Senior Interreligious Advisor
The American Jewish Committee
February 2001

Introduction

THROUGHOUT his visit to the Holy Land, Pope John Paul II prayed. He prayed publicly, ending many of his homilies and speeches by invoking God's help and blessings. He prayed silently, even as many looked on. And he prayed privately at the holiest of places. This book is a journey in prayer with Pope John Paul II, re-living his dramatic pilgrimage of March 20-26, 2000. For all that was said and written around the world about this trip—about the sensitive politics of the Middle East, about the places visited, about interreligious disputes—John Paul's pilgrimage was, in the end, about a man's prayer to God. This book approaches the events in that spirit.

John Paul wanted the world to follow with him as he journeyed through the history of salvation, sensing God's hovering presence in a special time and place. Before starting, he predicted it would be an emotional experience, and it was: "These have indeed been days of intense emotion," the pope said on the final day of his pilgrimage. "A time when our soul has been stirred not only by the memory of what God has done but by his very presence."

From the start, the story was full of drama. There was the aging, frail pope, returning near the end of his life to a land that had inspired him to write poetry when he visited the holy places as a young bishop. There was an almost crushing weight of history—the tragic past of Christian-Jewish relations, and of the Crusades. And the pope entered a web of politics, the interminable struggle between the Israelis and Palestinians. All of these elements made for a good story for the 2,000 journalists who covered the trip—when my colleague Bob Keeler and I were assigned to it, we knew this was an event people would want to read about.

But there was something more. If it were simply a story about a famous man, about politics, about history, it would not have fascinated people around the world to the degree it did.

But it was also a story about encountering God—about the pope, with all he is and all he represents, experiencing with all his remaining might the places where God entered human history. This is what led millions of people—the devout, the merely curious, the skeptical—to follow each day of John Paul's journey in the Holy Land.

Yet this element of the story was downplayed in many news accounts of the trip. Reporters searched for the bits of political or social commentary in homilies that were overwhelmingly about faith in God, and those snippets became the stories that were printed and broadcast around the world. Of course, the political story was important. There was the hope that perhaps John Paul, who hastened the downfall of European communism, could somehow encourage peace in the Middle East. And it's understandable that John Paul's religious themes would be submerged in the coverage: Eternal truths don't work well as breaking news. Reporters, after all, were writing for general audiences, for nonbelievers as well as believers. But in his homilies, John Paul left a wealth of thought and prayer that will endure, not only as history but as a way to reflect on God's presence in this very moment. This spiritual message was the core of Pope John Paul II's trip to the Holy Land, and it deserves to be recounted and reflected upon. This book quotes extensively from what he said, because it's worth pondering. And it describes the locations he visited, because the places have such power that they became like characters in this drama of the interaction between holy man and holy place. We're re-telling the story from a faith perspective.

The first time around, we covered the story for the newspaper *Newsday*, where Bob was the religion writer and I was the city editor who supervised coverage of New York City. We were pleased that the paper's editors agreed with our view that the trip should be seen primarily as a pilgrimage and not as a political mission. And so with our Middle East bureau chief,

Matthew McAllester, keeping watch for political fallout from the pope's visit, we were free to draw out the events' religious meanings.

We arrived in Jerusalem from New York a week before the papal visit to attend a conference, Religion and Media 2000+, that provided helpful perspectives by arranging meetings with such figures as the chief rabbi, the grand mufti, a local Catholic bishop and Cardinal William Keeler of Baltimore, who took part in the sessions. While we certainly knew each other through our work at *Newsday*, Bob and I weren't all that well acquainted, since Bob had worked throughout his career at the paper's main office on Long Island while I was based in New York City. We found we were kindred spirits in many ways. Both of us, we learned, grew up in the same general area in southern Brooklyn and both attended high schools run by the Catholic Diocese of Brooklyn. Both of us take seriously our roles as laymen in the Catholic Church, engaging in various parish ministries. Both of us have an interest in the Church's teachings on social justice. And we both were intrigued by John Paul, admiring him but unhappy with some of his decisions and with some directions the Vatican has taken during his papacy.

It was Bob's first trip to the Holy Land and my second—I had covered a trip the late Cardinal John O'Connor made throughout the region in 1992, a visit that helped smooth out the Church's relations with Israel. Naturally, we wanted to spend as much time as we could pondering the holy places, and, though jet-lagged and sleep deprived, immediately went to Jerusalem's Old City and promptly got lost in its twisted alleyways. Soon enough, we learned our way around and found ourselves in an unusual situation—two reporters who were both on assignment and conscious of being on a spiritual journey as well.

But once John Paul arrived and stirred up a revival among Christians in the Holy Land, our personal prayer pretty much ended. We worked constantly, skipping meals and getting little and sometimes no sleep. Whatever prayer or Scripture routines we had at home were set aside. Covering a papal trip is strenuous; for logistical and security reasons, reporters are required to be in place hours before an event—you don't just show up for a 10 a.m. Mass a few minutes ahead of time. It was also a highly competitive story, covered by media from all over the world. So our thoughts were focused on journalistic basics such as getting the key quotes, observing details, and meeting deadlines. In short, covering the trip was not a truly spiritual experience because we were unable, as the pope might say, to be docile to the workings of the Spirit.

At the same time, we felt the raw emotion of the events, the people, the places. We heard moving homilies each day and got a chance to feel the power the holy places impart. And so we kept journals, saved copies of all the pope's homilies, and looked forward to reflecting further at home.

Once we got back, I found that people I knew really wanted to hear about the trip, more so than for any other story I'd ever covered. Having told many a reporter's "war story" over the years about covering celebrated trials or other "talkers" (stories everyone's talking about), I noticed that friends, relatives, and fellow churchgoers listened with unusual attention when I related what happened on the pope's pilgrimage. My aunt, Marie Bradley, invited me to speak to her Renew group at St. Joseph's Church in Toms River, N.J. As an aid, I pulled together a handout that compiled the pope's prayers at such sites as Mount Nebo, Bethlehem, the Israeli Holocaust memorial, Nazareth, the Church of the Holy Sepulchre. While driving down the Garden State Parkway from my home in Brooklyn, I realized that this could be an outline for a book about the papal pilgrimage. And so this book was born out of a desire to help people to reflect in wonder on those seven days in the Holy Land. Writing this book has given us the chance to recollect in tranquility what we heard and felt as we watched John Paul trek across the history of salvation.

We've told the story in the way we experienced it, a day at a time, with one chapter for each of the trip's seven days. In order to cover as much of the pope's very busy schedule as possible for our newspaper, we leapfrogged each other, splitting the reporting. So, for example, while Bob braved the wind-blown sand as the pope prayed beside the Jordan River after covering an outdoor Mass in Amman, I was in Bethlehem, preparing to cover the events there. In the book, we've each written about the events we covered. Bob wrote the first two chapters, which cover John Paul's visit to Jordan. I wrote the third chapter, on the pope's day in Bethlehem, and so on, as noted in the chapter headings.

We've written the book in a way we hope will appeal to a wide audience. We especially hope that those who have distanced themselves from organized religion will find something worthwhile here. Simply put, John Paul said things that deserve to be heard, whether or not one believes he speaks with special authority as the Successor to Peter. While we would question him on such matters as how church authority is wielded or the role of women in the church, we also find his optimistic brand of Christian humanism to be inspiring and uplifting. Despite his expansive optimism, he seems to get much more attention when he says "No!" We hope this book will introduce people to a fuller range of his ideas.

In a sense, the pilgrimage gave flesh to the insights John Paul has poured out in his official writings, books, homilies, speeches, audiences, and poetry. His teachings have always focused on the Incarnation and Redemption, the Crib and the Cross, and from the outset of his papacy, he looked forward to celebrating these events in the year 2000. In his pilgrimage, he would travel to the places where those events occurred; word and deed would merge as he prayed beside the sites of Jesus' crib and crucifixion. These emotional scenes grew out of hopes John Paul expressed in 1979 in his first encyclical, *Redemptor Hominis* (The Redeemer of Man), in which he said that the jubilee celebration in 2000 "will recall and reawaken in us in a special way our awareness of the key truth of faith which Saint John expressed at the beginning of his Gospel: 'The Word became flesh and dwelt among us,' and elsewhere: 'God so loved the world that he gave his only Son, that whoever believes in him should not perish but have eternal life.' "[1] From the start, his face was set toward Bethlehem and Jerusalem, toward Crib and Cross.

As the third millennium after Jesus' birth drew closer, the pope began to disclose plans to celebrate "the key truth of faith" by going on pilgrimage to the Holy Land in the year 2000. In his 1994 letter *Tertio Millennio Adveniente*, he spoke of preparation for the year 2000 as a "key of my Pontificate,"[2] the way to understand his years as pope. Separating his millennial fervor from the hysteria of the Y2K doomsday crowd, he wrote about why the passage of time is sacred to Christians, quoting a passage from Paul's letter to the Galatians: "When the fullness of time had come, God sent forth his Son, born of woman." "The fullness of time," he explained, "coincides with the mystery of the Incarnation of the Word . . . and with the mystery of the Redemption of the world."[3] It is when "Eternity entered time," when God became human. Since the history of salvation has unfolded through time, he wrote, measurements of time—hours, days, years, centuries—are "imbued with the presence of God."[4]

Humankind has always tried to re-create the sacred events of the past in the present through festivals and rituals.[5] John Paul's ambition to make the most of the Great Jubilee Year of 2000 by savoring the divine presence reflected a drive ingrained in the hearts of all who are religious, across many ages, cultures, and faiths. A real appreciation for time's passage requires something more than party hats, champagne, and worship of a glass ball dropping in Times Square.

In that same 1994 letter, John Paul wrote of his "fervent wish" to visit the Holy Land. "It would be very significant if in the Year 2000 it were possible to visit the places on the road taken by the People of God of the Old Covenant, starting from the places associated with Abraham and Moses,"[6] he wrote. One reason his pilgrimage so resonated with people of many faiths was that the pope showed a keen sense of how both time and place can be sacred. Even in a secular age, human beings yearn to be religious—often without realizing it—and appreciation for sacred spaces and times is at the heart of the religious experience in many eras and cultures. In a 1999 letter that detailed his plan to visit "places linked to the history of salvation," John Paul explained how a place can become holy.

"At first sight," he wrote, "it may seem puzzling to speak of precise 'spaces' in connection with God. No less than time, is not space completely subject to God's control?" Despite their ancient tradition of pilgrimage to the Holy Land, Christians have always been ambivalent about the idea that places can be holy because of their belief that God is within. As the pope put it: "God is equally present in every corner of the earth, so that the whole world may be considered the 'temple' of his presence."

But, the pope continued, "Just as time can be marked by . . . special moments of grace, space too may by analogy bear the stamp of particular saving actions of God." It is, again, a basic human need. "This is an intuition present in all religions, which not only have sacred times but also sacred spaces, where the encounter with the divine may be experienced more intensely than it would normally be in the vastness of the cosmos," he wrote.

Reality "unveils itself" where there is a sense of connection between heaven and earth; human beings need holy places because they are brought close to the divine and to the world as it was "when it came fresh from the Creator's hands."[7] To put it another way, the visit of a religious leader of the pope's depth and fame to the holy places in a holy year was bound to create an excitement growing out of a deeply held human need to connect with the sacred. Trained in his younger days as an actor, playwright, and poet, John Paul has always had a gift for using language, symbol and setting to create moments of epiphany for an audience. He understands that any good story about a trip is never just about traveling from place to place, but an allegory for journeying through life toward under-standing and meaning. His pilgrimage would be an interior journey, not only for himself, but for all willing to join him through the extensive coverage the trip was sure to get.

In his 1999 letter, John Paul repeated poetry he'd written years earlier after his 1963 pilgrimage to the Holy Land, show-ing how the primary purpose of his trip was to be transformed within by the places he encountered. He wrote: "I come across these places which you have filled with yourself once and for all. . . . Oh place . . . You were transformed so many times before you, His place, became mine. When for the first time He filled you, you were not yet an outer place; you were but His Mother's womb. How I long to know that the stones I am treading in Nazareth are the same which her feet touched when she was Your only place on earth. Meeting You through the stone touched by the feet of Your Mother. Oh, corner of the earth, place in the holy land—what kind of place are you in me? . . . I will take you and transform you within me into the place of new testimony. I will walk away as a witness who tes-tifies across the millennia."[8] Even then, he was looking to the threshold of the next millennium.

And so, despite age, infirmity, and Mideast political ten-sions, John Paul was determined to return to the Holy Land in the year 2000. He cleared away diplomatic obstacles, nudging the Vatican bureaucracy to recognize Israel's statehood. He worked his way through Israeli-Palestinian political disputes that many said might prevent his trip because of the Vatican's long-standing support for Palestinians, some of whom are Catholics.

He made clear from the start that it would be a spiritual journey, not political or diplomatic, writing that he would be "saddened" if other meanings were attached to the trip. Of course, politics and religion don't detach so easily, especially in the Middle East, and so every step of his trip was shadowed by the possibility that he would offend the Israelis and Jewish religious leaders, the Palestinians, Muslims, Orthodox Christians, and even Arab Catholics who felt deprived of attention from the Western church. In particular, John Paul and Church officials took great pains to balance the trip's schedule fairly between the Israelis and Palestinians.

In addition to going on a spiritual pilgrimage, the pope was hoping to encourage the local Christians—the "living stones" often overlooked by pilgrims—and stem their exodus from the Holy Land. He also hoped his trip would help soothe differences with the Orthodox Christian churches, which had a long and bitter history of disputes with the Catholic Church over control of the holy places. And he aimed to create dialogue among Muslims, Jews, and Christians by emphasizing their common heritage as children of Abraham. But most of all, he wrote, he wanted "To go in a spirit of prayer from one place to another, from one city to another, in the area marked especially by God's intervention." This, he wrote, "helps us not only to live our life as a journey, but also gives us a vivid sense of a God who has gone before us and leads us on, who himself set out on man's path, a God who does not look down on us from on high, but who became our traveling companion."[9]

John Paul had hoped to begin his travels in Abraham's native city of Ur in modern-day Iraq, but was unable to do so because of political complications. In February, 2000, he traveled to Egypt to pray at Mount Sinai, following in Moses' footsteps. He returned to the Vatican and then the following month resumed his excursion through salvation history by visiting the peak of Mount Nebo in Jordan, the place where Scripture says Moses viewed the Promised Land.

Before him lay the land where he liked to say God had "pitched his tent," a literal translation for John's poetic descrip tion of Jesus' birth, that "the Word was made flesh and dwelt"—pitched his tent— "among us." But in reality, his pilgrimage had begun before he left Rome and did not end when his plane departed from Tel Aviv on March 26, 2000. "Indeed," he wrote months before the trip began, "spiritually I am already on this journey, since even to go just in thought to those places means in a way to read anew the Gospel itself; it means to follow the roads which Revelation itself has taken."

So Bob and I welcome you to join us on this journey, to go "in thought" to a holy land with Pope John Paul II.

—Paul Moses

Chapter 1

Mount Nebo

Arriving in Jordan for the start of his historic pilgrimage to the Holy Land—the first by any pope since 1964—Pope John Paul II exchanged greetings at the airport with King Abdullah II of Jordan, expressing profound hopes for peace in this troubled region. Then his motorcade took him to Mount Nebo, to stand where Moses stood when he viewed the Promised Land after forty years of leading his people through the desert. Bob wrote this chapter.

The Prayer

Here on the heights of Mount Nebo I begin this stage of my Jubilee pilgrimage. I think of the great figure of Moses and the new Covenant which God made with him on Mount Sinai. I give thanks to God for the ineffable gift of Jesus Christ, who sealed the Covenant with his blood and brought the Law to fulfillment. To him who is "the Alpha and Omega, the first and the last, the beginning and the end" (Revelation 22:13), to him I dedicate every step of this journey which I make through the Land which was his.

The Place

On Sunday, March 19, the day before Pope John Paul II was to fly into Jordan for the first stop on his pilgrimage, Paul and I left Jerusalem for the capital city of Amman, on a bus filled with religion writers and journalism students from Columbia University in New York.

We were all traveling together as part of a conference called Religion and Media 2000+. For several days in Jerusalem, we had listened to speakers on the maddeningly complex situation in the Middle East, met with political and religious leaders, familiarized ourselves with the city, and worked to get ready for the pope's arrival. On this sunny Sunday morning, after Cardinal William Keeler of Baltimore had offered Mass for the group, we climbed on a bus in front of our hotel and headed for Amman.

After a three-hour bureaucratic delay at the Allenby Bridge, a major border crossing between Israel and Jordan, two nations technically at peace, I found myself wondering how long it would have taken to cross the border if they had never signed a peace treaty in 1994.

As we neared Amman, our Jordanian guide, Osama Twal, told us about the ancient forebears of today's Jordanians, the Moabite, Ammonite, and Edomite kingdoms. In the city, it became obvious that Jordan, a land steeped in ancient history, is trying very hard to be modern. Just as easily as he had rattled off facts about Jordan's antiquity, "Sammy" pointed proudly to evidences of the nation's modernity, such as a McDonald's and a Kentucky Fried Chicken.

The archaeological evidence[1] shows that people have been living in the area of Amman for 9,000 years. The Greeks called it Philadelphia and the Hebrews knew it as Rabbah of the Ammonites. To my eyes, however, many of the buildings looked as though the workers had laid the last desert-hued stones in place barely a week before we arrived. History bears out my impression. The city in its current form has sprung up in the past fifty years.

As recently as 1948, the year after the United Nations General Assembly voted to partition Palestine and create the Hashemite Kingdom of Jordan, the city's population was only 25,000.[2] A large influx of Palestinian refugees from the 1947-1949 Arab-Israel war started Amman's growth spurt. The Six-Day War in 1967 and the Gulf War in 1991 also brought major influxes of refugees. By 2000, the population of greater Amman was beyond 1.5 million and climbing toward two million.

That population growth has spread the city geographically and fueled a continuing construction boom. In less than a decade, the number of hotel rooms[3] doubled, soaring past 12,000 in 1997. We could see evidence of that growth clearly in the late Sunday afternoon sun, as the bus finally reached our hotel, the Grand Hyatt. Right across the street, we saw what we learned would become another hotel, a massive round building rising toward the sky, evoking images of the tower of Babel.

The construction of a new luxury hotel right across the street from the Grand Hyatt offered evidence of Jordan's drive for modernity. It also seemed a bit imprudent, to say the least, given a 1999 report describing the average hotel occupancy rate in Amman[4] as the lowest in any Middle Eastern country, less than 52 percent.

The low occupancy rate was only one symptom of a nettlesome reality: The signing of the Israel-Jordan peace treaty had not yet produced the economic boom that Jordanians had expected. The nation was experiencing double-digit unemployment, partly the result of the influx of expatriates after the Gulf War and the surplus of skilled labor. Our guide told us he works seven different jobs to make a living. That pattern, I gathered, was typical in Jordan.

In that troubled economic context, many Jordanians hoped that John Paul's visit would bring a long-term boost in tourism. Everywhere he went on this religious pilgrimage, the pope would face similar unrealistically high expectations for political or economic profit from his journey. In his 1999 letter describing his planned trip to the Holy Land, John Paul seemed to anticipate those unruly hopes. "It would be an exclusively religious pilgrimage in its nature and purpose, and I would be saddened if anyone were to attach other meanings to this plan of mine,"[5] he wrote.

This was not a journey about political gain or tourism or unemployment, but a pilgrimage to the actual places in this dry, sometimes harsh corner of the world where God chose to work out so much of the history of human salvation. John Paul is a man shaped by his sense of geography and history, by the agonies of the Polish nation, by the rhythms of small-town life in Wadowice, by the intellectual ferment of Kraków, long before he learned the complex bureaucracy of Rome. This is a pope of many places, the most widely traveled pope of them all. Profoundly aware of the significance of place in the divine economy, he has made it a hallmark of his pontificate to kiss the earth of each new land that he visits for the first time. On this trip, he turned his eyes intensely on the places of the Holy Land—places brought vividly to life by sacred texts and by centuries of faith, places transformed from mere points on a map into markers of eternity.

A few minutes after we had checked in at the hotel and dropped off our luggage in our rooms, we scrambled back on the bus for a late-afternoon trip to one of those places of pilgrimage, Mount Nebo, where Moses stood to view the Promised Land. We knew that only a small pool of reporters would be allowed on these historic heights the next day, Monday, when the pope arrived. We were anxious to see what he would see, while we were still permitted to see it.

By the time we got there, the late March sun was about to set. In a way, the delay at the Allenby Bridge, followed by a long lunch in Amman before we had reached the hotel, turned out to be useful. If we had arrived in the flat light of afternoon instead of the soft glow of dusk, the view west, beyond the northern shore of the Dead Sea toward the glistening skyline of Jerusalem, would not have been nearly as striking. In that sense, we were seeing a grander sight than John Paul himself would see.

But we didn't have much time to view it. In minutes, the mountaintop would be closed to the public, and the security that surrounds every papal journey would clamp down. The lateness of the hour added a sense of urgency to Sammy's narrative. As we stood, looking west toward Jerusalem, Sammy rattled off a hurried torrent of facts. Near us, toward the western edge of the mountain, stood a striking sculpture by Giovanni Fantoni of Florence.[6] It is shaped like a cross, with a serpent winding itself sinuously toward its top, a reminder both of the Crucifixion and of the bronze serpent that Moses placed on a pole at God's command and held up before his people to cure them of snake bites. The sculpture evokes John's Gospel, where Jesus draws a parallel between his impending death and the story of the great Hebrew prophet and lawgiver: "And just as Moses lifted up the serpent in the wilderness, so must the Son of Man be lifted up, that whoever believes in him may have eternal life."[7]

Whether Moses stood on the exact spot where we were listening to Sammy, or whether it was a few feet or several hundred yards away, it was clear that we were seeing essentially what he saw, and we were standing at the place where the pope would be standing in less than 24 hours. The pope was coming here as a pilgrim, one in a long line of Christian pilgrims to this place sacred to the memory of the great prophet of the Israelites. The very name of the actual peak where we stood, Jabal Siyagha in Arabic, testifies to the centuries of pilgrimage to these heights. Siyagha means monastery, and there was a monastery here at least as early as AD 394,[8] when a Roman pilgrim named Egeria visited. What she saw was a memorial that the early Christians had erected to Moses. In the sixth century, a larger church went up on the same site.

Since 1933, Franciscan friars[9] have been conducting archaeological explorations at Siyagha, and the Franciscan Custody of the Holy Land continues to work toward restoration of the memorial of Moses inside the sixth-century church. A temporary roof covers the church, to protect the centuries-old mosaics that we were now hastily viewing, and to make it serviceable for liturgies. In a few hours after our visit, John Paul would be kneeling in prayer among those mosaics, beneath that roof.

At the end of our too-brief stay, we got back on the bus and rode in the gathering darkness to Madaba, the most heavily Christian city in this predominantly Muslim kingdom. It is a busy market town that also enjoys a long history as the location of a renowned mosaic school. In this "City of Mosaics," the most famous mosaic of them all is a map of the Holy Land, spread across the floor of St. George's Greek Orthodox Church.

As we entered the church with Sammy, I didn't get the sense of its significance, perhaps because the church does not surround the Madaba Map with the intense security that a treasure of comparable eminence would command in the United States or Europe. As Sammy stepped around the edges of the map to point out its features and explain its history, I kept thinking that no tour guide would be allowed to approach so close to this treasure if it adorned the floor of a cathedral in Florence or New York. But then, this is Sammy's town, and he is known and trusted here.

The map, created in the sixth century,[10] was not discovered until 1896, during the construction of this church, on the site of an earlier church. It depicts the entire region, from the Mediterranean to Jordan, with Jerusalem and its Church of the Holy Sepulchre at the center. During the construction, workmen destroyed sections of this precious map. Still, its more than two million stone cubes provide so much detail about Jerusalem and the rest of the Holy Land that archaeologists have often used this map for guidance in finding ancient sites.

Outside the church, it was clear that Madaba was more than ready for the papal visit the next day. In the center of town, busy Baladiya Circle was so festooned with lights that it looked like Christmas in March. Even though the pope's itinerary did not even call for a stop in the town, he would be rolling through it. That was enough to give birth to a group of committees that worked hard for weeks to spruce up Madaba.

Here, as elsewhere in the region, the pope's visit was an important morale boost for Christians. Though they are the majority in Madaba, they are a tiny minority in Jordan. In the Holy Land itself, controlled by the Israeli government and by the Muslim-dominated Palestinian Authority, the numbers of Christians have been dwindling. Many, especially the wealthy and highly educated, have been leaving the region. So, for those who remain, John Paul's visit would be a significant rallying point, a reason for hope and optimism in the Christian community.

The morning after our visit to Mount Nebo and Madaba, we met at our hotel with Prince Hassan Ben Talal, the brother of the late King Hussein and the uncle of the new king, Abdullah II. Throughout the kingdom and the region, the widespread expectation had once been that Prince Hassan, a man of great learning and immense charm, would someday follow his brother to the throne. Instead, Hussein had chosen his son as his successor. Now Prince Hassan continues his work of building bridges to other faiths. In that capacity, he told us that the pope's visit was "hugely courageous" and that it would bring moral authority and vision to the region. "For me, and for many, many others," he said, "it is a visit of hope."

A few minutes after our meeting with Prince Hassan ended, most of our group boarded the bus for the return trip to Jerusalem. Paul got on the bus, and I stayed behind, with a small handful of reporters from other papers, to cover the start of the pope's visit to Jordan a few hours later. Since I was not in the pool for the trip to Mount Nebo, I had to do what so many reporters find themselves doing so often on papal trips: I covered it by television from the press center in Amman, grateful that we had at least been to the mountain and to Madaba, so I could understand something of what the pope was about to experience.

The pope's plane touched down on the tarmac at Queen Alia Airport outside Amman at 2 p.m. Within minutes after his arrival, in a ten-minute speech at the airport, Pope John Paul II made clear that it was the spiritual significance of places of pilgrimage that had brought him to Jordan.

"My visit to your country and the entire journey which I am beginning today is part of the religious Jubilee Pilgrimage which I am making to commemorate the Two Thousandth Anniversary of the Birth of Jesus Christ," John Paul told King Abdullah and a glittering gathering of public officials and the influential of Jordan. "From the beginning of my ministry as Bishop of Rome, I have had a great desire to mark this event by praying in some of the places linked to salvation history—places that speak to us of that moment's long preparation through biblical times, places where Our Lord Jesus Christ actually lived, or which are connected with his work of redemption. My spirit first turned to Ur of the Chaldeans, where Abraham's journey of faith began."

What John Paul did not say, but we all knew, was that the complex situation in Iraq, where Ur is located, had prevented the pope from visiting the site in person. So his pilgrimage to Ur, where the patriarch Abraham first heard God's call, could only be a pilgrimage in spirit. Politics had deprived him of the rich experience of steeping himself in that place.

"I have already been to Egypt and Mount Sinai, where God revealed his name to Moses and entrusted to him the tablets of the Law of the Covenant," the pope continued. "Today I am in Jordan, a land familiar to me from the Holy Scriptures: a land sanctified by the presence of Jesus himself, by the presence of Moses, Elijah and John the Baptist, and of saints and martyrs of the early Church."

Though his spirit was fixed on the role of this land in salvation history, John Paul showed that he clearly understood its travails in modern times. "In this area of the world there are grave and urgent issues of justice, of the rights of peoples and nations, which have to be resolved for the good of all concerned and as a condition for lasting peace," the pope said. "No matter how difficult, no matter how long, the process of seeking peace must continue. Without peace, there can be no authentic development for this region, no better life for its peoples, no brighter future for its children. That is why Jordan's proven commitment to securing the conditions necessary for peace is so important and praiseworthy.

"Building a future of peace requires an ever more mature understanding and ever more practical cooperation among the peoples who acknowledge the one true, indivisible God, the Creator of all that exists. The three historical monotheistic religions count peace, goodness and respect for the human person among their highest values. I earnestly hope that my visit will strengthen the already fruitful Christian-Muslim dialogue which is being conducted in Jordan, particularly through the Royal Interfaith Institute."

In this brief talk at the airport, the pope struck a delicate, carefully nuanced balance between affirming the essentially religious nature of his pilgrimage and expressing acute, sympathetic awareness of the political turbulence that grips the region. Again and again during his stay in the Holy Land, John Paul demonstrated a nimble ability to maintain that balance, without taking sides.

From the airport, the pope's motorcade went to Mount Nebo. A little more than an hour and a half after his plane had touched down at the airport, John Paul walked slowly, leaning on his cane, into the sixth-century church that we had visited on Sunday evening. Kneeling at a prie-dieu in the central aisle, John Paul closed his eyes in prayer for several minutes, showing once again his ability to pray even in the most clamorous circumstances, with every eye and every camera focused on him."

At this historic moment on the mountaintop, the camera did not miss even the tiny cut on the right side of the pope's forehead, an injury that he had sustained in a collision with a bookshelf just two days before leaving for Jordan. For all his immense power of will, his iron determination, John Paul has slowed visibly in recent years, his body worn down by a near-fatal assassination attempt, illness, accident, and age. His frailty has made him a living symbol of both human mortality and the power of human will.

After this brief respite of silence, the pope sat down, put on his stole and led a short prayer. Then one of the Franciscan friars read briefly from the Book of Deuteronomy, the familiar account of the last days of Moses, his view of the Promised Land from Mount Nebo, and God's decision not to allow Moses to cross into the Promised Land himself. The pope listened, led in the recitation of the Our Father, then said a few words to those gathered with him in the ancient church.

"Here on the heights of Mount Nebo I begin this stage of my Jubilee pilgrimage," John Paul said. "I think of the great figure of Moses and the new Covenant which God made with him on Mount Sinai. I give thanks to God for the ineffable gift of Jesus Christ, who sealed the Covenant with his blood and brought the Law to fulfillment. To him who is 'the Alpha and Omega, the first and the last, the beginning and the end' (Revelation 22:13), to him I dedicate every step of this journey which I make through the Land which was his."

After greeting the Franciscans and the officials of Madaba, the pope concluded with this blessing: "May the blessings of the Almighty be upon the people of the area! And may the peace of heaven fill the hearts of all who join me on my pilgrim path!"

Then the pope sat and greeted a long line of children and nuns, handing each a rosary, as a group of children sang the triumphal hymn of the kingship of Jesus, *"Christus vincit, Christus regnat, Christus, Christus imperat."* The children broke into chants of "John Paul II, we love you," and "John Paul II, God bless you." The pope appeared to draw energy from them, as he always does when he is surrounded by the young. As the Franciscans began leading him on a brief tour of the ancient church, he stopped to bless a plaque commemorating his visit.

Following his half hour in the church, John Paul walked outside, past Giovanni Fantoni's striking serpentine cross and up a few steps to the place where he was to view the Promised Land as Moses did. The pope hung his cane on the railing, then looked westward in silence, gazing intently at the Holy Land, which was draped in a slight haze beneath the bright afternoon sun. Surrounded by cameras, reporters, and a small crowd of Franciscans and Jordanian public officials, the pope maintained his silence, taking in the view and remaining alone with his thoughts, standing essentially where Moses stood and seeing very much what Moses saw.

© AP/WIDE WORLD PHOTOS

On the first day of his visit, Pope John Paul II looks reflectively toward what Moses called the Promised Land.

Reflection

Beyond John Paul's momentary presence in this place so deeply associated with Moses, the parallels between this modern-day pope and the ancient prophet are striking.

Moses came to this mountaintop at the end of a 40-year journey, an old man leading a "stiff-necked people," a description that God himself first used for them in Exodus 32:9, and a term repeated often in the Hebrew Scriptures and again in the Book of Acts. John Paul arrived at Mount Nebo at the start of one pilgrimage, his long-awaited visit to the Holy Land, but nearing the end of the broader pilgrimage of life. Like Moses, he is old, and like Moses, he leads a people that he clearly regards on occasion as stiff-necked and difficult. Throughout his long papacy, he has not hesitated to point an admonishing finger at the world's one billion Catholics, curbing what he thought were the excesses of liberation theology, warning the people in the pew about the culture of death, and decrying the materialistic culture of the West, just as Moses fought against his people's urge to worship a golden calf.

Like Moses, who in his final days offered his people a long review of the law and a song of praise to the God who was denying him entry to the Promised Land, the pope in his old age has been producing a succession of definitive documents, such as the one rejecting the ordination of women. Many Vatican watchers see those documents as a twilight summary and reiteration, designed to remind the pope's stiff-necked people of where he and the Church stand, as he nears his own end.

The prophet and the pope have both been great teachers and lawgivers. Jews affectionately call their greatest prophet *Moshe rabbeinu*, Moses our teacher. John Paul has shared something of that role, with his stupendous output of teaching documents and his stern adherence to law. Both men have given us intensely cinematic lives to contemplate—lives so full of rich, improbable, and grace-filled moments that they absolutely had to become movies.

Moses floated in the reeds as an infant; grew up in the pharaoh's court; slew an Egyptian who was mistreating a Hebrew; escaped from Egypt; met God on the mountaintop; returned to challenge the pharaoh; led his people across the sea and into the desert; brought forth water from a rock; carried the tablets of the commandments down from the mountain, and struggled with the feeble faith of the Israelites for forty years.

John Paul lost his whole family before he was 21; survived the Nazi bombing of Kraków; worked in a stone quarry to avoid deportation to a concentration camp; disobeyed Nazi edicts and committed the capital offenses of attending a secret seminary and participating in an underground theater; nearly died when a German truck ran him down; learned to function as a priest and a young bishop in the repressive communist regime that controlled Poland after the war; won election to the papacy at age 58; helped launch the Solidarity movement in Poland that set off the downfall of European communism; survived an asssassin's bullet, and became the most widely traveled pope in history.

The two men also offer strong contrasts.

Moses was a reluctant prophet. Just before he encountered the burning bush on Mount Horeb, he was doing nothing more bold and prophetic than tending the sheep of his father-in-law, Jethro. So, when Moses approached the burning bush and heard the voice of God promise to lead him and his people out of bondage in Egypt, he did not exactly leap to the task. Like all the great prophets of Hebrew Scripture, he did not see himself as gifted enough or brave enough for the mission, but he was canny enough to grasp the difficulty of the thankless job that God was offering, and to protest his unworthiness.

"Who am I that I should go to Pharaoh, and bring the Israelites out of Egypt?"[11] Moses asked.

God reassured him that he would not be alone in this difficult undertaking, but Moses clearly remained skeptical about God's promise of help. So Moses sought a little token of God's authenticity, a piece of inside information that would help him prove to the Israelites that he really was a prophet speaking for God, and not just a man who had stayed out too long in the sun on the mountaintop. He asked for God's name.

"God said to Moses, 'I am who I am.' He said further, 'Thus you shall say to the Israelites, 'I AM has sent me to you ' "[12]

This is a profound moment in salvation history,[13] when God utters his name—in Hebrew, *"ehyeh asher ehyeh,"* meaning "I am that I am." (God's proper name, derived from this assertion, became Yahweh. In all the centuries since Moses posed that cheeky question to his creator, the Jewish people have stood so in awe of God's name that they avoid uttering it. They say *Adonai,* meaning Lord, or *HaShem,* The Name. But they seldom say *Yahweh.*) Still, even the thunderous significance of this moment did not erase the doubts of Moses, who plowed ahead with his objections.

"O my Lord, I have never been eloquent, neither in the past nor even now that you have spoken to your servant; but I am slow of speech and slow of tongue,"[14] Moses argued. Reassured that God would give him the words to say, Moses finally accepted the divine commission, but without notable enthusiasm.

In sharp contrast, John Paul has never shown signs of reluctance to embrace his prophetic mission. Enduring significant hardship to become a priest, he grew vigorously and unhesitatingly into that priesthood, then became a bishop at the age of 38. Moses had to stand up to pharaoh for a short time, but the young bishop, Karol Wojtyla, boldly opposed the communist leadership of his country for two decades. Then, returning to Poland in triumph as pope in 1979, he helped inspire and nurture the Solidarity movement that led his people to freedom from the totalitarian power he had fought for so long as a priest and a bishop.

Moses may have been a stammerer, as many scholars have deduced from his argument to God that he was slow of speech and slow of tongue. But John Paul brought to the papacy astonishing linguistic gifts, not only in his native Polish but also in a breathtaking array of foreign languages. He has written a long list of books, encyclicals, apostolic exhortations, and other printed communications. And when he appears in public around the world to speak, he displays not only a mastery of language but also a sure-footed actor's feel for the moment and the audience.

Whatever powers of language he can summon up, John Paul has placed them at the service of what he called in the ancient church on Siyagha "the ineffable gift of Jesus Christ." From the start of his pontificate, in the 1979 encyclical *Redemptor Hominis* (The Redeemer of Man), he has adopted as a central theme his joy in Jesus and in the human dignity that the Incarnation confirmed beyond all doubt. Here on Mount Nebo, more than two decades after he obeyed the Vatican bureaucrats who urged him not to make the immediate pilgrimage to the Holy Land that his heart had longed for, John Paul was gazing for his first time as pope at the land where that ineffable gift once walked the streets and the hillsides.

The pope was here precisely because he understood something fundamental about these places where his journey was finally taking him. More than contested coordinates on a map of modern conflict, these places were pivotal points in the unfolding, immensely human mystery of Incarnation. God, the eternal and transcendent reality beyond time and space, had chosen to enter human history most definitively in these hills and valleys, these rivers and deserts, this land promised to Moses but ultimately denied to him.

That ultimate disappointment offers another striking contrast between the reluctant prophet and the pilgrim pope: Moses did not get to see the Promised Land. John Paul did.

At the start of his pontificate, when he was still young and full of vigor, John Paul proposed a simple but stunning plan: He should travel to Bethlehem for his first Christmas as pope. On the level of evangelization, spreading the Gospel by deed as well as word, this seemed like an unassailable idea. Diplomatically and logistically, the crusty Vatican bureaucracy argued, it would have been a perilous venture. So they told the new pope not to go. "For one of the few times in twenty-one years, John Paul let his evangelical instincts be trumped by the ingrained cautiousness of his diplomats,"[15] wrote George Weigel, the pope's biographer, in a diary of the Holy Land visit. Over and over, when they discussed the Middle East, the supreme pontiff would ask his aides: "When will you let me go?"

For more than two decades after that first planned journey ran aground on the rocks of caution, John Paul cherished his desire to visit the Holy Land. He had also developed a strong sense that God wanted him to lead the Church into the new millennium. Under his leadership, the Vatican developed immensely complicated and ambitious plans for the Jubilee Year 2000, and John Paul had every intention of leading those events, despite his debilitating health problems. With his immense power of will, he transcended age and frailty to bring himself to the top of Mount Nebo and look out to the Promised Land. One day later, he would board a plane and fly to Israel. The prophet did not cross the Jordan. The pope did.

Questions for Reflection

1. How have Christians been a "stiff-necked people," like their elder brothers in the faith, the Jews?

2. If we had the chance to speak directly with the pope, as the Israelites could grumble directly to Moses about manna delivery, what reason would we find for complaint?

3. If we were in the place of either the prophet or the pope, how would we cope with the faithlessness of our people?

4. What can we learn from the persistence Moses and John Paul showed, despite illness, frailty, disappointment and old age?

5. How has a sense of place enriched your spirituality?

Chapter 2

Amman: Mass at the Soccer Stadium

The pope began his day with a helicopter ride to the soccer stadium in downtown Amman, where he offered Mass in gray and drizzly weather. In the afternoon, the helicopter took him to the Wadi al-Kharrar, a riverbed leading to the Jordan River. Many believe that this was the place where John the Baptist baptized Jesus. Following a brief, windblown prayer service at the wadi, John Paul got back into the helicopter, flew to the airport outside Amman, and left for Israel. At Ben-Gurion International Airport, he began his high-profile visit to Israel with the Hebrew greeting of peace, "Shalom!" That simple act of courtesy and respect for tradition drew wide comment, warmed hearts, and launched his stay in Israel on a positive note. Bob wrote this chapter.

The Prayer

However impossible it seemed, Isaac was born to Sarah, and Abraham received a land. And through Abraham and his descendants the promise became a blessing to "all the families of the earth" (Genesis 12:3; 18:18).

That promise was sealed when God spoke to Moses on Mount Sinai. What passed between Moses and God on the holy mountain shaped the subsequent history of salvation as a Covenant of love between God and man—a Covenant which demands obedience but promises liberation. The Ten Commandments etched in stone on Sinai—but written on the human heart from the beginning of creation—are the divine pedagogy of love, indicating the only sure path to the fulfillment of our deepest longing: the

34

human spirit's irrepressible search for goodness, truth and harmony.

The Place

Like so many other places where John Paul has celebrated a huge outdoor Mass, the soccer stadium in downtown Amman did not itself provide any spirituality of place. The day before, Mount Nebo had evoked palpable images of the prophet Moses. Now, the soccer stadium practically echoed with past grunts of exertion and groans of defeat, in games all wrapped up with national pride. Bathed in the cool drizzle falling from a heavily overcast sky, this plain, utilitarian concrete bowl seemed like anything but a holy place.

Of course, the stadium did have the essential architectural element for a papal Mass: a huge temporary structure that elevated the altar and sheltered it from the elements. A large banner proclaimed: "Vatican Jordan Friendship Nobility." The sound system droned a long biography of the pope, then an announcement: Someone had parked a car on the helicopter pad where the pope would soon land, and the owner needed to move it.

In this dreary setting, my eyes welcomed the colorful presence of about 2,000 elementary school children, all wearing white robes and yellow stoles, the Vatican colors. Each wore a wooden cross, with today's date inscribed, and carried a candle reverently in hands folded for prayer. These children, it turned out, were here to receive their first Holy Communion. Many of them had awakened at 5 a.m. or earlier, in order to be there on time.

As they waited patiently for the pope's arrival, the crowd began rehearsing a variety of cheers. "Abdullah II, John Paul II, God bless you," they chanted. That didn't have a lot of rhythm, but this Arabic chant did: "*Marhaba, marhaba, marhaba al-baba.*" It means nothing more than "welcome, welcome, welcome to the pope," but its rhythm stuck with me for days after-ward. And on the scoreboard, this electronic exhortation flashed in English, with the Arabic beneath: "Open your doors to Christ."

John Paul arrived in the stadium a little after 8:30, and the entrance procession for the Mass started about 20 minutes later. The liturgy lasted just over two hours, and in that time, I saw some odd sights.

Moments after the pope's 21-minute homily had ended, I watched little yellow-and-white groups of the new communicants drifting away from their seats on the floor of the stadium. That was the first time I had ever seen that at any Mass, let alone a papal Mass. As I watched them and thought about it, the reason became clear: They had already been in the cool, drizzly stadium far longer than the average new communicant spends at Mass, and they needed bathrooms badly. On top of that, they had just listened to a homily entirely in English, but most of them spoke only Arabic.

At the kiss of peace, in the stands right in front of me, I witnessed an unfolding scene that fell far short of peaceful. Throughout the Mass, small knots of people had been trying to work their way past the ushers to climb down the stairs leading from the upper stands to the floor of the stadium. The ushers resisted, and at the kiss of peace, one of them started yelling angrily at those who were trying to reach the stadium floor.

Normally, I refrain from interviewing anyone during a liturgy, but I had to find out what was causing this bizarre scene. With the help of my translator, a young American-educated Jordanian woman named Reham Fakhoury, I asked an usher what all the commotion was about. He explained: Some people thought that, if they got closer to the altar, they'd be able to receive Communion from the hands of the pope himself—as if that somehow made the Real Presence more valid or meaningful. The organizers had apparently not sufficiently briefed the congregation about one of the inescapable realities of a papal liturgy: Only a small, pre-selected group of people gets to receive Communion from the pope. Everyone else receives from the priests spreading through the crowd.

So, like any outdoor papal Mass that I had ever attended, this one offered distractions that made focusing on the liturgy itself difficult. The pope's words, rather than the place, had to provide the meaning. His homily had to bring significance to the moment.

The pope began it with the inevitable verse from Isaiah: "A voice cries out: In the wilderness prepare the way of the Lord! Make straight in the desert a highway for our God!" (Isaiah 40:3). Then he offered the greeting of peace in Arabic and started his homily, focusing heavily on John the Baptist, the patron saint of Jordan.

"We look for a guide to show us the way," John Paul said. "And there comes to meet us the figure of John the Baptist, a voice that cries in the wilderness. . . . Guided by him, we make our journey of faith in order to see more clearly the salvation which God has accomplished through a history stretching back to Abraham. John the Baptist was the last of the line of Prophets who kept alive and nurtured the hope of God's People. In him the time of fulfillment was at hand.

"The seed of this hope was the promise made to Abraham when he was called to leave all that was familiar and follow a God he had not known (Genesis 12:1-3). Despite his wealth, Abraham was a man living in the shadow of death, for he had no son or land of his own (Genesis 15:2). The promise seemed a vain one, for Sarah was barren and the land was in other hands. But still Abraham put his faith in God; 'he believed, hoping against hope' (Romans 4:18).

"However impossible it seemed, Isaac was born to Sarah, and Abraham received a land. And through Abraham and his descendants the promise became a blessing to 'all the families of the earth' (Genesis 12:3; 18:18).

"That promise was sealed when God spoke to Moses on Mount Sinai. What passed between Moses and God on the holy mountain shaped the subsequent history of salvation as a Covenant of love between God and man —a Covenant which demands obedience but promises liberation. The Ten Commandments etched in stone on Sinai—but written on the human heart from the beginning of creation—are the divine pedagogy of love, indicating the only sure path to the fulfillment of our deepest longing: the human spirit's irrepressible search for goodness, truth and harmony."

The arc of the homily culminated in Jesus, standing at the Jordan and submitting to baptism. "Jesus is the realization of the promise," the pope said. "His death on the Cross and his Resurrection lead to the definitive victory of life over death." At the end of his homily, John Paul addressed bishops, priests, nuns and mothers (it was Mothers' Day in Jordan), and brought it all back to Jesus and to the children who had waited so long in the drizzle. "And to the children making their First Holy Communion, I say: Jesus is your best friend; he knows what is in your hearts. Stay close to him, and in your prayers remember the Church and the Pope."

Reflection

The pope began with a verse from the prophet Isaiah, which Luke's Gospel cites in describing the desert ministry of the fierce and fearless prophet John the Baptist, the herald of the messiah. John was the son of a priest named Zechariah and his wife Elizabeth. She was both a descendant of Aaron, the brother of Moses, and a relative of Mary, the mother of Jesus.

The readings and the pope's homily offer us a vision of two decent men of God who have trouble transcending the apparent tyranny of the facts, in order to accept the reliability of God's promises and the power of God's commands.

Abram, the great patriarch called forth from Ur of the Chaldeans and later renamed Abraham, heard God's promise to lead him to a new land and make of his descendants a great nation. That seemed very unlikely to Abram, because he and his wife Sarai had shown no ability to bear children. As for the land, as John Paul put it, "the land was in other hands." The pope's delicate little phrase strikes me as an echo of the whole maddeningly intractable mess in the Middle East, which grew even more violent and difficult in the months after the pope's visit to the Holy Land. Thousands of years after God's command to Abram to leave his own country and go to the land possessed by the Canaanites, some of the descendants of Abram now hold that land, but to other descendants of the patriarch, the Palestinians, the land appears to be "in other hands."

At the moment when God asked the childless Abram to go forth, establish a great nation and take possession of the land for them, Abram uttered a very human doubt: "O Lord God, how am I to know that I shall possess it?"[1] In strikingly similar words, the simple Hebrew priest Zechariah questioned the angel's revelation that Elizabeth is to bear a son. "How will I know that this is so?"[2] Neither man seemed to believe in the possibility of posterity at that stage of his life.

For his lack of faith in God's promise, Zechariah lost the power of speech. Months later, at the birth of his son, the relatives questioned Elizabeth's plan to name the baby John, an uncommon name in that family. Still unable to speak, Zechariah wrote on a tablet: "His name is John."[3] Then his voice returned and he sang a canticle of praise for God's saving action, the "Benedictus," which Catholics recite every day in the Liturgy of the Hours, the church's universal prayer.

One of the greatest Catholic Scripture scholars, the late Rev. Raymond E. Brown, believed that Zechariah did not compose this eloquent piece of poetry spontaneously. Rather, Brown argued,[4] it came from a group of Jewish Christians, steeped in the spirituality of the *anawim*, Hebrew for the poor ones, who had no strength of their own, but had to rely on the saving power of God. Whatever its origins, Luke found this canticle appropriate for Zechariah and appended it to the infancy narrative.

"He has raised up a mighty savior for us in the house of his servant David, as he spoke through the mouth of his holy prophets from of old, that we would be saved from our enemies and from the hand of all who hate us,"[5] Zechariah proclaimed.

For his fidelity to the divine call, of course, John the Baptist ultimately paid with his blood. This price was common among the prophets, as John Paul emphasized in his homily, but God was honest with them about the cost of fearless prophecy. At the very start of Jeremiah's difficult career of telling truth to power, God warned him that the kings, the princes, and the people themselves would fight against him. To shore up Jeremiah's courage, God promised to stand by his prophet and deliver him.[6]

For something like four decades, Jeremiah did not hesitate to criticize caustically the southern kingdom of Judah and its capital Jerusalem, which fell to the Babylonians during Jeremiah's lifetime, about six centuries before the birth of Jesus. So biting were Jeremiah's words about the sinfulness of the kingdom of Judah that the prophet's name became the root of an English noun, "jeremiad," meaning "a prolonged lamentation or complaint" and "a cautionary or angry harangue."[7]

The pope's visit to Mount Nebo evoked images of the pope and the prophet Moses as two persistent old men leading a stiff-necked people. His homily in the soccer stadium, rich in references to the prophets, reminds us of the prophetic dimensions of his pontificate. Like Jeremiah and John the Baptist, his words have not always made a welcome sound in the ears of the powerful, the kings, the presidents, and the dictators.

American Catholics are most familiar with his wily and steadfast opposition to the evils of communism, the second of the tyrannies that shaped his life. In a country that has spent more than a half-century developing a reflexive anti-communism as a central element of the national character, we easily applaud him for this. We willingly accept theories that the 1981 attempt on his life was not the work of one man, but the result of a communist-led conspiracy to silence him. But we tend not to pay as much attention to the pope's critique of our own nation's culture and economy.

Even in the years after the fall of communism in Europe, John Paul did not accept capitalism unreservedly. He examined the post-communist reality in his 1991 encyclical, *Centesimus Annus*, written on the 100th anniversary of Pope Leo XIII's social encyclical, *Rerum Novarum*. The question he posed was this: whether, in the passing of communism, it was fair to say that "capitalism is the victorious social system, and that capitalism should be the goal of countries now making efforts to rebuild their economy and society?" His answer was, in essence: not so fast. There is capitalism and there is capitalism, the pope was saying. He could not endorse a capitalism that lacks boundaries, a capitalism without "a strong juridical framework which places it at the service of human freedom in its totality."[8]

In his critique, John Paul did not go as far as those who see "savage capitalism" as a new form of idolatry. The golden calf in this secular cult is the free market itself, a benevolent deity whose devotees believe it will always deliver the right results, so long as the political system allows it to operate without interference. But the pope did say, in effect, that any honest analysis of economic systems has to include a wary approach to capitalism.

With similar wariness, the pope has expressed reservations about the dimensions of freedom in American society, where it is a pivotal concept in the national self-image. John Paul sees freedom essentially as liberty to choose the morally good. In the United States, he clearly believes, freedom has sometimes descended into license to choose whatever is desirable.

Nor has John Paul always accepted America's view of world affairs. During the Gulf War, far from anointing the coalition that President George Bush assembled to eject Iraqi troops from Kuwait and defend Saudi Arabia, the Vatican argued that the coalition had not exhausted diplomatic approaches to the crisis before opting for an overwhelming military solution that devastated the entire Iraqi nation for decades to come.[9]

Somehow, we miss those dimensions of his prophetic stance, just as we seem not to hear his sharp rejection of capital punishment, an unnecessary barbarity that sets America apart from the rest of the developed world. Perhaps we do not adequately hear him speaking truth to power on these issues, because we focus so much on his higher-volume condemnation of the culture of death in America, where abortion-on-demand has been elevated to the status of a sacred principle. American journalists have a sharp ear for John Paul's stand on abortion, so constantly repeated that no reasonable person could call it news, but they make much less fuss about his positions on war and peace, economic justice and the death penalty.

Nonetheless, his homily in Amman, the capital of a nation whose patron saint is the great prophet John the Baptist, offers us an opportunity to reflect on the prophetic nature of John Paul's ministry. This is a pope who does not see the Ten Commandments as burdensome, but as "the divine pedagogy of love," a pope unafraid, like Jeremiah and John the Baptist, to stand at the gates of the mighty and speak the truth.

Wadi al-Kharrar

The Prayer

Let us pause in contemplation on the banks of the Jordan, this sacred place in the history of salvation.

Here, the chosen people passed over to the Promised Land. Here, John performed his baptism of repentance. Here, the holy theophany, the manifestation of the Trinity, took place at the baptism of Jesus. As we recall that event with gratitude, let us call to mind our own baptism and bless the Father, the Son and the Holy Spirit.

The Place

Soon after the Mass and a brief stop at the press center, we boarded the bus for the trip west from Amman toward the Jordan River. What we found was a wide-open, windy sweep of arid land, covered with parked buses. As we hiked from our bus toward the wadi itself, I began feeling the relentless cloud of fine sand that the cool wind drove into our faces and our clothing.

The Wadi al-Kharrar, a riverbed leading down to the Jordan, is just one contender for the title of the true site where John the Baptist baptized Jesus. Not far away, on the west bank of the river, in an area still controlled by the Israelis, is another site, the Qasr al-Yahud, favored by the Palestinian Authority as the actual baptismal site. Though the Palestinian Authority does not yet control Qasr al-Yahud, it hopes to gain that control some day. So the Palestinians were elated to learn that the pope, in an effort at even-handedness typical of his approach to the entire pilgrimage, would visit both sites—the Wadi al-Kharrar today and the Qasr al-Yahud tomorrow.

In the dispute over the legitimacy of the two sites, the stakes are high for the governments in this region, which want to attract tourists and the money they will spend. At the moment, neither site has much in the way of amenities for pilgrims. Like the nearby Dead Sea, both sites are among the lowest places on earth, more than 1,000 feet below sea level, and both suffer from temperatures well above 100 degrees in the summer. Both have been at the heart of modern-day military struggles between Israel and its neighbors. Qasr al-Yahud, the scene of terrorist activity after the Israelis won control of the West Bank in 1967, remains under Israeli military control today, and pilgrims have only occasional access to the site. Since the Israel-Jordan peace treaty of 1994, the Wadi al-Kharrar is out of the field of conflict. But it is situated in Jordan, which means that pilgrims to the holy places in Israel must go through the tedious bureaucracy at the Allenby Bridge border crossing before they can even approach this site.

No mass transportation or modern highway system provides access to the Wadi al-Kharrar, and no permanent facility offers pilgrims a place to rest, eat, and study the history of the area. Eventually, however, the Jordanian government plans to build a visitors' center, a John the Baptist research center, and other facilities here.

The Jordanian government hopes that these facilities will help attract a steady stream of pilgrims to a site that lay at the center of pilgrimage routes from the beginning of Christian times. Those visits, documented as early as the fourth century and continuing throughout the first Christian millennium, constitute a powerful argument that the baptism of Jesus took place at the Wadi al-Kharrar site. The Gospel of John itself makes a strong case for a baptismal site on the far side of the Jordan from the world that Jesus knew in Galilee and Jerusalem: "This took place in Bethany across the Jordan where John was baptizing."[10]

That Bethany, of course, is not to be confused with the Bethany that lies just outside Jerusalem, a village known in the Gospels as the home of three close friends of Jesus: Lazarus and his sisters, Martha and Mary. One of the best known events in the life of Jesus, the raising of Lazarus from the dead, took place in the Bethany near Jerusalem.[11] The other Bethany, east of the Jordan, came to be known in the early Christian era as

Bethabara, Hebrew for "house of the crossing,"[12] because this was where both Joshua and the prophet Elijah crossed the Jordan. It was in this same area that Elijah was ushered into heaven by a whirlwind and fiery chariots drawn by fiery horses.[13] For many centuries, tradition has situated that event on a hill known in Arabic as Tell Mar Elias, right here at the head of the Wadi al-Kharrar. So the site evokes dual associations with Elijah and John the Baptist.

Beyond the textual evidence provided by the words of Scripture and the memoirs of pilgrims, another powerful argument for the authenticity of the Wadi al-Kharrar is its unfolding array of archaeological evidence. Those artifacts have only become available since the 1994 peace treaty between Jordan and Israel and the removal of the land mines that had created a lethal barrier between the opposing armies. All along the southern edge of the Wadi al-Kharrar, a stretch of less than two miles leading down to the river itself, archaeologists have found a rich variety of sites, including a monastery, hermitages, churches, and baptismal pools. Most of the major structures seem to have been built in the fifth and sixth centuries, but archaeologists have also found smaller artifacts, such as coins and pottery, that date back to the pre-Christian era.[14]

The complementary evidence of Scripture and archaeology are embodied in Muhammad Waheeb, a Muslim archaeologist who carries around the Christian Scriptures in both Arabic and English. He and others believe that the actual baptism of Jesus may not have taken place in the Jordan River, which lies in a deep gorge and is subject to periods of flooding and muddiness, but in the freshwater springs flowing down from the Wadi al-Kharrar to the Jordan.

Wherever that pivotal moment of salvation history unfolded, it is difficult to imagine more than a few hundred people gathered around the rough-hewn prophet John the Baptist. As my translator, Reham, and I reached the site, thousands of peo-

ple had already arrived. Hundreds sat beneath a tented pavil-
ion flanking the actual place where the pope was to lead a brief
prayer service. On a slope across from that site, thousands
more stood waiting. We took our seats in a section set aside
mostly for the press, perhaps fifty yards from a stone arch over
the site where the pope would pray.

The helicopter carrying the pope set down just after 3:30,
and less than twenty minutes later, he arrived in a golf cart at
the altar set up for this brief prayer service. Without his white
zucchetto, which would have flown away instantly in this
intense wind, John Paul's thin white hair blew freely in the
breeze. His aides placed a stole around his shoulders, and one
held a microphone to his face as the pope began to pray. The
wind whipped the canvas of the tent, making it difficult for us
to hear him.

At the Wadi al-Kharrar, a bracing wind and thousands of people greet John
Paul.

Reflection

"Let us pause in contemplation on the banks of the Jordan, this sacred place in the history of salvation," John Paul said at the start of the brief liturgy. "Here, the chosen people passed over to the Promised Land. Here, John performed his baptism of repentance. Here, the holy theophany, the manifestation of the Trinity, took place at the baptism of Jesus. As we recall that event with gratitude, let us call to mind our own baptism and bless the Father, the Son and the Holy Spirit."

The pope leaned on his crozier and fell silent for a moment, then resumed his prayer. "Blessed are you, Lord, all-powerful God," he said. "In Christ, the living water of salvation, you granted us every blessing and made of us a new creation. Almighty God, almighty Father, in the holy signs of our faith, you renew the great events of creation and redemption."

As John Paul prayed, two altar servers with white cassocks and yellow stoles poured water from two small jars into a larger jar resting in a flowered stand near the pope. "Bless this water and grant that those who were reborn in baptism may be witnesses and heralds of the Easter which is constantly renewed in our church," he said. "We ask this through Christ our Lord. Amen."

The pope stood, leaning on his crozier, during the Arabic proclamation of Luke's Gospel, the story of John the Baptist and the baptism of Jesus. Then he sat down and offered a brief homily and greeting:

"In the Gospel of St. Luke we read that 'the word of God came to John the son of Zechariah in the wilderness; and he went into all the region about the Jordan, preaching a baptism of repentance for the forgiveness of sins' (3:2-3). Here, at the River Jordan, where both banks are visited by hosts of pilgrims honoring the Baptism of the Lord, I too lift up my heart in prayer:

'Glory to you, O Father, God of Abraham, Isaac and Jacob!

You sent your servants the Prophets
to speak your word of faithful love
and call your people to repentance.
On the banks of the River Jordan,
you raised up John the Baptist,
a voice crying in the wilderness,
sent through all the region of the Jordan
to prepare the way of the Lord,
to herald the coming of Jesus.

'Glory to you, O Christ, Son of God!

To the waters of the Jordan you came
to be baptized by the hand of John.
Upon you the Spirit descended as a dove.
Above you the heavens opened,
and the voice of the Father was heard
'This is my Son, the Beloved!'
From the river blessed by your presence
you went forth to baptize not only with water
but with fire and the Holy Spirit.

'Glory to you, O Holy Spirit, Lord and Giver of life!

By your power, the Church is baptized,
going down with Christ into death
and rising with him to new life.
By your power, we are set free from sin
to become the children of God,
the glorious Body of Christ.

By your power, all fear is vanquished,
and the Gospel of love is preached
in every corner of the earth,
to the glory of God,
the Father, the Son and the Holy Spirit,
to whom be all praise in this Jubilee year
and in every age to come. Amen.' "

Then he stood, dipped branches into the blessed water and prayed: "Let this water call to mind our baptism in Christ, who has redeemed us with his death and resurrection." The pope led the assembly in the Our Father, offered a closing blessing, and ended the service with this prayer: "May St. John the Baptist protect Islam and all the people of Jordan, and all who participated in this celebration, a memorable celebration. I'm very grateful to all of you. Thank you very much."

Only a half hour after the service had begun, the pope climbed in his golf cart, gently kissed someone's baby, then rolled off toward the helicopter, accompanied by mounted soldiers in uniforms trimmed with bright red. (Why is it, I wondered, that even men of peace are supposed to feel honored by the presence of the military, whose entire purpose is waging war? Wouldn't the pope have felt just as honored, say, by a group of Jordanian school crossing guards?)

Within a few minutes, long before our bus had even returned us to the press center in downtown Amman, the pope would be boarding a jet at Queen Alia Airport for the flight to Israel. At that end, Paul would cover the arrival ceremony. Out of touch with those developments, I took a long cab ride back to the Allenby Bridge, in the company of John Rivera, a religion writer for *The Baltimore Sun*. (Looking at the map afterward, I realized we had been very close to the Allenby Bridge at Wadi al-Kharrar, but we had to ride all the way back east to Amman in order to catch the cab that would take us back west to the crossing point.) At the border, we endured another frustrating wait, then caught a second cab back to Jerusalem. Arriving at my room in late evening, I sat down to write my share of the day's events.

It had been a very long day, starting with a 3:30 wakeup and followed by a cab to the press center, a bus to the soccer stadium, a bus to the baptismal site and the long return to Jerusalem. But the tedious logistics of travel and the pressure of deadlines did not deprive me entirely of a pilgrimage experience.

At the Wadi al-Kharrar, breathing in the sub-sea-level air and feeling the sharp welcome of the sand against my face, I had experienced something important in my own spiritual life. On Mount Nebo, I had felt strongly that I was seeing what Moses saw, but Moses himself is still a distant figure to me—a great prophet, but not a great presence in my daily life. At the baptismal site, I experienced something much deeper and more personal: a powerful sense of what the long journey to this place must have felt like for Jesus, our great brother.

Though the day of John Paul's visit was cool, the desert wind summoned for me images of what this stark landscape might have been like in the heat of summer. I could imagine vividly the difficulty that Jesus would have encountered in making the long walk south from Nazareth, sweating profusely in the sun and wind, as the drifting sand clung to his every pore. Though the Gospel accounts make clear that he did not choose his first disciples until after his baptism by John and his forty days of solitude in the desert, my imagination kept conjuring up a scene with the glorious knuckleheads who agreed to put their occupations on hold and follow Jesus everywhere. Suppose he had chosen them *before* the baptism and asked them to walk with him the great distance from Nazareth to Bethany beyond the Jordan, so that he could meet with a smelly, highly excitable relative, dressed in camel's hair and surviving on locusts and wild honey? In today's patterns of speech, they would probably have asked him something like this: "And the purpose of that would *be*?"

The purpose, of course, was to undergo baptism, a rite of repentance. As Christians, we believe that Jesus himself, free from sin, had no need of repentance. In fact, the Rev. Daniel J. Harrington, the eminent Jesuit scholar, believes that this is a strong argument for the historicity of the baptism. [15] The early church would hardly have included in the Gospel this story of Jesus undergoing an unnecessary baptism unless it had actually happened. In fact, Matthew's account of the event may well reflect the church's embarrassment over the apparent contradiction of Jesus, the sinless one, submitting to a ritual of forgiveness. Matthew has John the Baptist protest: "I need to be baptized by you, and do you come to me?" And he reports Jesus as answering: "Let it be so now; for it is proper for us in this way to fulfill all righteousness."[16]

Before my visit to the Wadi al-Kharrar, these words would summon up one sort of image, pale and formless. But my few hours in that desert place blazed up my imagination and filled it with more sensory perceptions—the feel of the sand, the smell of the air, the sound of the wind, the colors of the soil. St. Ignatius Loyola, the founder of the Society of Jesus, advocated a meditation on Scripture that fully immerses the senses in the story. That day taught me that this imaginative meditation process can be so much more powerful if you have experienced the place where the story unfolds. At the Wadi al-Kharrar, I found myself untroubled by my long-cultivated journalistic skepticism, which prompts me always to wonder whether any historical site is located at the exact latitude and longitude of the events it recalls. The arguments for the Wadi al-Kharrar seem persuasive, but I didn't really feel that it mattered whether the baptism took place here, or a short distance away, on the western bank of the Jordan. My brief time at the wadi gave me an overwhelming sense of the place where Jesus was baptized, of the desert where he spent his next forty days on retreat, praying over the painful months that awaited him.

My time in this stark place, followed later in the week by a long, pleasant automobile ride from Nazareth to Jerusalem, gave me a visceral sense of the long, dry walk that Jesus took from Galilee to the wadi. My few hours in the wind brought vivid new meaning to the familiar phrase, "the howling wilderness," and helped me to imagine his gritty time alone in the desert. Together, these invigorated, highly sensory images taught me something compelling about the strength of personality that Jesus brought to his ministry. My little imaginative reconstruction of Scripture, in which Jesus asked his new friends to accompany him to the baptism, did not actually happen. But if it had, my wadi-enhanced sense of Jesus tells me, they might have expressed hesitation, but they would have followed him across the Jordan and into the desert.

This strengthened sense of the personality of Jesus, gained through a physical experience of a place, turns me back to something that John Paul said in his prayer at the wadi: "Here, the holy theophany, the manifestation of the Trinity, took place at the baptism of Jesus." Though it doesn't come up in everyday conversation, theophany is a lovely word lifted directly from the Greek—yet another example of the charming covetousness of the English language, always willing to steal shamelessly whatever it needs, regardless of the source. Theophany sounds abstruse and impenetrable, but means nothing more complex than this: a manifestation of God.

The thing to remember about theophanies is that they don't always feature the Spirit of God descending in the form of a dove, with a heavenly voice announcing: "This is my Son, the Beloved, with whom I am well pleased."[17] Theophanies come in all sizes, shapes and colors. They dress as friends, and they wear the guise of enemies. They issue from the mouths of Christians, but they can just as easily emanate from Jews, Buddhists or Muslims. (Notice, for example, that the pope prayed that St. John the Baptist would protect Islam. The Muslims have much to teach us about the transcendence of God and the importance of regular prayer. In the years ahead, one of the greatest challenges for John Paul and his successor will be the dialogue with the Muslim world.)

Our God is a tricky God, peeking out shyly from behind the commonest of daily occurrences, operating through the unlikeliest of agents, hinting vaguely at obscure purposes, leading us cagily in directions we couldn't have imagined, for reasons yet to be revealed. Certainty is elusive, and most of us have to spend our lives working to discern what God is saying to us in the events and the people we encounter. Our faith assures us that our God moves always among us, nudging us toward a reign of justice and peace, but it is difficult to figure out what any theophany may be saying—or whether it is really a theophany at all.

In the chill wind of the Wadi al-Kharrar, I like to think, it is possible that I experienced a little theophany: a small insight into the personality and strength of Jesus. This much I can say for certain: At the very least, I collected the most meaningful of my Holy Land souvenirs, a small sample of desert sand. Clinging tenaciously to the royal blue wool of the Mets cap that I wore to the baptismal site that day, the sand reminds me vividly of the desert wind that Jesus braved to reach his own historic theophany near the banks of the Jordan River. I can't think of a more useful souvenir than that.

Questions for Reflection

1. In our own lives, have there been moments when God has called us to speak out prophetically against evil, as he called the prophet Jeremiah, or called us to leave behind the life we know, as he called Abram in Ur of the Chaldeans?

2. Have we resisted a calling because we see something as impossible, as Abram and Zechariah doubted their ability to have children, even in the face of God's promise?

3. What favorite Scripture stories blaze up our imaginations, and what texts leave us cold?

4. How can we engage these difficult texts with greater imagination?

5. What theophanies have we experienced in our lives, and how have we discerned whether they were really appearances of God or our own stubborn wills lurking in disguise?

Chapter 3

Bethlehem: Mass in Manger Square

Traveling by helicopter, John Paul started his day by squeezing in a brief trip to a second possible location for John's baptism of Jesus, located on the West Bank of the Jordan River. Then he was flown by helicopter to Bethlehem, where the Palestinian Authority welcomed him at the helipad. In a ceremony, Palestinian Authority President Yasser Arafat and other officials and religious leaders greeted the pope. That was followed by Mass in Manger Square, private prayer in the Grotto of the Nativity and a visit to the Dheisheh refugee camp. Paul wrote this chapter.

The Prayer

O Child of Bethlehem, Son of Mary and Son of God, Lord of all time and Prince of Peace, "the same yesterday, today and forever" (Hebrews 13:8): as we set forth into the new millennium, heal all our wounds, strengthen our steps, open our hearts and minds to "the loving kindness of the heart of our God who visits us like the dawn from on high" (Luke 1:78). Amen.

The Place

Manger Square in Bethlehem is bound by a collection of souvenir stores and offices that have sprung up near the sixth-century Church of the Nativity, built above the traditional site where Jesus was born. Recently refurbished, it fairly sparkled in comparison to the way it looked in earlier years, providing an intimate setting for the papal Mass. After celebrating Mass,

55

Pope John Paul II entered the church, which is under Greek Orthodox jurisdiction, arriving through a portal leading from the adjacent Church of St. Catherine, a Catholic church. The Nativity church was built by Emperor Constantine in the fourth century, then destroyed in a revolt in 529 but later rebuilt. It is not a graceful-looking building; it is, as the pope said in his homily, like a "fortress." But part of its attractiveness is that it has survived many centuries of turbulence, unlike other ancient churches in the Holy Land, which were repeatedly destroyed and rebuilt. A legend holds that Nativity church was spared in a Persian invasion in 614 because of a painting of the magi, who were dressed in Persian clothing. Today, pilgrims line up to duck into a low doorway designed to discourage attackers; there is no grand entrance.

The pope followed the pilgrims' path down a stairway and through a door the Crusaders built to enter the grotto of the Nativity. He knelt in prayer for about five minutes beside the 14-point silver star set in white marble beneath an altar on the spot where tradition holds Jesus was born of Mary, as indicated in the Latin inscription, *Hic de Virgine Maria Jesus Christus Natus Est.* Then he stepped down to the site of the manger, requested his breviary (which contains The Liturgy of the Hours, daily readings from the Psalms) and a chair and asked to be alone. The fifteen or so people who had accompanied him into the grotto retreated and John Paul prayed in solitude for about a quarter-hour.

It's interesting to note that the same grotto extends beneath the Church of St. Catherine (although blocked off by a black metal door through which one can look into a keyhole), where the rocky limestone walls remain, preserving the original cave and the sense of what it might have looked like in Jesus' day.

Many leading scholars, particularly Catholic experts, dispute that Jesus was born on this site. They liken the infancy narratives in the Gospels of Luke and Matthew to a *midrash,* stories the rabbis told to illuminate spiritual truths. But there is a very old tradition passed down from early Christians that this was in fact the place where Jesus was born. Early Christian literature such as the *Protoevangelium of James*, which is not in the Bible, speaks of Jesus' birth occurring in a cave near Bethlehem. (The Bible does not mention a cave.) In AD 135, when the Romans occupied Bethlehem after squelching a Jewish rebellion, Emperor Hadrian established a shrine to Adonis above such a grotto. There is a tradition, cited by St. Jerome in the fourth century, that it was done to prevent Christians from venerating the site.

Reflection

It is perhaps odd that Pope John Paul's beautiful homily in Bethlehem, which is very much a Palestinian village, should remind me of the tragic fate of an Orthodox Jewish man in my hometown, Brooklyn. But given the homily's universality, it's appropriate that a message aimed in part at comforting the Palestinian people should somehow make me think of a 29-year-old Hasidic scholar, Yankel Rosenbaum.

He had the misfortune to be walking the streets of Brooklyn's Crown Heights section shortly before midnight on August 19, 1991. In the heat of that summer night, a bitter anger seized a mob of people in the streets after a 7-year-old boy, Gavin Cato, was killed on the sidewalk by a car that went out of control. It wasn't just any car—it was part of the police-escorted entourage of the late, renowned leader of the Lubavitch Hasidic sect, Rabbi Menachem Mendel Schneerson. And the victim was yet another black child in a summer when so many had died. A mob formed, exhorted to "Get a Jew."

Rosenbaum was stabbed with a knife and, soon after, taken to city-run Kings County Hospital Center. New York City Mayor David Dinkins quickly showed up at Yankel Rosenbaum's bedside to show his concern. Rosenbaum's wound did not appear to threaten his life. But the staff at Kings County, where the lives of so many victims of violence had been saved, made an awful mistake. While Rosenbaum was treated for one puncture on the right side of his chest, the staff failed to notice another wound on the left side. Yankel Rosenbaum bled to death.

I always thought that the failure to see Rosenbaum's wounds was a metaphor for the cause of what followed. Rioting went on for four days before confused city officials finally put an end to it. Finger-pointing went on for at least two more years—until Mayor Dinkins was voted out of office—as a wave of anger swept through the Jewish community over the way the city responded to the riots.

The root of all the anger, it seemed to me, was that both the black and the Jewish communities suffered with the feeling that no one could *see their wounds*. The mayor's presence at the dying man's bedside seemed only to heighten the terrible apt-ness of the metaphor. (But I don't mean to disparage Mayor Dinkins, who was trying to cope with a very difficult situation.)

Wherever he's traveled, John Paul has seen the wounds and made his vision of them part of his spiritual message. For to see a person's hidden wounds is to recognize the innate dignity that results from being made in God's image. The dignity of each human being is a key theme for John Paul, one that reach-es a high point in Bethlehem, the place where God entered human history in the person of Jesus. Because of the Incarnation, he has written, "the nature shared by all human beings is raised to a sublime dignity."[1]

There is no better place to celebrate this than in Bethlehem, where, as the pope said, it's Christmas every day. A visitor feels the Incarnation, whether it be in sweeping views of the Shepherd's Field, the pine and palm trees in Manger Square, the carved wooden bells and creches and mother-of-pearl stars in the souvenir shops, or the Church of the Nativity.

From the moment of his arrival in the Palestinian territories, John Paul tended to the wounds. He did so with the simple papal gesture of kissing a bowl of soil brought before him. (Because of the possible political implication, this touched off a minor hysteria among some at the press center in Bethlehem where I viewed the arrival ceremony on a TV feed. I was surrounded by several French reporters who wanted to know if I had spotted the pope kissing the bowl raised to him, and when I responded that he had, they shouted among themselves in French that "He kissed it! He kissed it!" I don't think there was much political significance to the gesture, but it gave the Palestinians something they craved—recognition of their dignity as a people. Later, the pope's spokesman, Joaquin Navarro-Valls, said: "It would be very strange if the Holy Father didn't kiss earth from the land where Jesus was born.")

Immediately afterward, the pope recognized the Palestinians' wounds—a theme he would build on throughout his day in Bethlehem. "No one can ignore how much the Palestinian people have had to suffer in recent decades," he said. "Your torment is before the eyes of the world. And it has gone on too long."

Then he added: "The Holy See has always recognized that the Palestinian people have the natural right to a homeland." That statement became the lead paragraph in many newspaper stories around the world, but if you look at it closely, it was not really news—as the pope indicated, he was repeating a position the Vatican had always held. John Paul had used almost the same words in his 1984 letter *Redemptionis Anno*, referring to the Palestinians' "natural right in justice to find once more a homeland." Nonetheless, it certainly touched a chord among the Palestinians, who interpreted it as support for their statehood.

After that brief ceremony with Palestinian Authority President Yasser Arafat and his wife, Suha, John Paul was taken to Manger Square in Bethlehem on a route that overlooks the slopes where Christian tradition holds that angels told shepherds to fear not. The streets, cleared of cars and secured for the papal visit, were blessedly quiet that morning after days of frantic preparation. In the Square, it was Christmas in March: the altar was flanked along one side by tall pine trees, and the congregation sang the angels' song: *"Gloria In Excelsis Deo."*

John Paul had longed to celebrate Mass in Bethlehem. He'd been there as a young bishop in 1963 and celebrated the Eucharist at the site of the Nativity on the night of December 8-9 from midnight until 5:30 a.m., when Greek Orthodox monks arrived for their liturgy. It must have made a great impression.

The scene of the papal Mass at Manger Square.

As he began his homily at the Mass in Bethlehem's Manger Square, he told the congregants that soon after he became pope in 1978, he sought to celebrate midnight Mass on Christmas in Bethlehem. "That was not possible then, and has not been possible until now," he said, without detouring into a discussion of how his request must have stunned Vatican functionaries—the Holy See at the time had no formal diplomatic relations with Israel, which had taken control of the West Bank of the Jordan River, where Bethlehem is located and many Palestinian Christians lived.

The people gathered before the altar, which had a huge, streaking Star of Bethlehem above and an array of yellow and white flowers below, saw the drama in the moment and broke out in applause. And it was a dramatic moment. So many people had questioned whether John Paul would live to see the new millennium he'd fervently spoken and written about throughout his papacy. So much had been written about his fading health, his apparent case of progressive Parkinson's disease. So much had been said about whether international diplomacy would permit John Paul to travel to the Holy Land. And yet, there he was, late in his life, back in Bethlehem— thanks to God, he made clear: "How can I fail to praise the God of all mercies, whose ways are mysterious and whose love knows no end, for bringing me, in this year of the Great Jubilee, to this place of the Savior's birth?"

It was as if he'd always been meant to stand on that altar in the little town of Bethlehem in the year 2000. "Bethlehem is the heart of my Jubilee pilgrimage," he declared. "The paths that I have taken lead me to this place and to the mystery that it proclaims."

In a sense, Manger Square could be the center of any tourist town, surrounded as it is with souvenir shops and municipal offices. But the Church of the Nativity, having survived the ravages of time and of conquering armies that destroyed all the other ancient churches in the Holy Land, reminds us that this place is unique for Christians because of the "mystery it pro-claims." Its stone walls loom, large and gray, to one side of the square.

The sense one gets from being in a holy place wasn't obscured by the awkwardly political decor. Palestinian flags were festooned everywhere with the gold-and-white Vatican flag, criss-crossing the square over the congregants' heads. Huge posters of a beaming Arafat shaking hands with the pope were hung on buildings behind and above either side of the altar. The same picture was everywhere—even on the Palestinian Authority press credentials that dangled from my neck.

The attempt to politicize has drawn many a scathing remark from American and Israeli commentators, but I think the Palestinian Authority's need to showcase its aspirations so blatantly was just another example of this people's insecurity. The Palestinians were sharing the world stage with a revered leader who loved them and shared their hopes, and their leadership was overly anxious to make the most of that. Indeed, it seemed a struggle for the fledgling Palestinian Authority to manage an event of such magnitude. The PA, as it is called, didn't seem quite ready for prime time. Logistics for reporters were a mess; I ended up walking miles to get in and out of Manger Square because of foul-ups with press buses that were supposed to pick up journalists at a hotel on the outskirts of town. (But what better place to walk than above these famous hills?) Security, compared to Jordan and Israel, seemed quite loose and easygoing. But if the pope minded, it didn't show. His standard acknowledgment to local authorities must have rung sweetly in their ears: "I am grateful to the officials of the Palestinian Authority who are taking part in our celebration and joining us in praying for the well-being of the Palestinian people."

By this time, John Paul had completed his introduction and the crowd assembled for Mass in Manger Square, somewhat restless to that point, became quieter. Those paying the closest attention were Arab Christians, so used to being a small minority in the Holy Land and to feeling forgotten in the Christian world. I've heard them called the "Cinderellas of the church." Now, they were invited to the ball, and here was the pope, speaking directly to them.

He spoke, first, of joy. For Bethlehem is the wellspring of John Paul's here-and-now optimism: "The joy announced by the angel is not a thing of the past. It is a joy of today—the eternal today of God's salvation, which embraces all time, past, present and future."

I liked that: "the eternal today." God envelops time and gives meaning to it—through Bethlehem, where God entered human time and space in the person of Jesus. Right there, across the square from a town hall where the officials wrangle about budgets and jobs, as they would in every town. Or, as John Paul put it: "At the dawn of the new millennium, we are called to see more clearly that time has meaning because here Eternity entered history and remains with us forever."

His message could have stopped on that point, a meditation on living the joy of Christmas year-round and on the promise of a new millennium. That would have been perfectly acceptable, but John Paul cut deeper, recognizing the suffering of the land he was visiting and linking it to Jesus' own circumstances. "The Savior was born in the night—in the darkness, in the silence and poverty of the cave of Bethlehem," he said.

Then he spoke of the Mass's first reading, Isaiah 9: "The people who walked in darkness has seen a great light; upon those who dwelt in the land of gloom a light has shone. You have brought them abundant joy and great rejoicing. . . . For the yoke that has burdened them, the pole on their shoulder, and the rod of their taskmaster you have smashed."

In the midst of a triumphant arrival in Bethlehem for the Jubilee Year marking 2,000 years since the Incarnation—"the heart of my Jubilee pilgrimage"—John Paul might well have preached only of the "great light" that Christ's birth brought to the world. To do so, though, would have been to ignore the faces looking at him, seeking answers to the conflict that gripped this land. The Incarnation means our prayers must be made flesh.

"This," he said, "is a place that has known 'the yoke' and 'the rod' of oppression. How often has the cry of innocents been heard in these streets? Even the great church built over the Savior's birthplace stands like a fortress battered by the strife of the ages."

Given the place and the audience, these were strong remarks. For the Palestinian people, many of whom were driven from their land in 1948, bottled up on the West Bank and arid Gaza and bypassed by the global economic boom, felt very much oppressed. The streets of Bethlehem had been filled with strife in recent years—even the Vatican-run Bethlehem University, a short distance from Manger Square, had been shut down by the authorities for three years in the late 1980s in an attempt to stem the rock-throwing uprising called the *intifada*. The pope's message was at once universal and very specific to the people gathered there that chilly, overcast March morning to hear him: "The Crib of Jesus lies always in the shadow of the Cross. The silence and poverty of the birth in Bethlehem are one with the darkness and pain of the death on Calvary." In his humanity, Jesus shared our suffering, from cradle to grave. He sees our wounds.

Where, then, can healing be found?

Jesus did not offer a political fix, the pope implied: "His kingdom is not the play of force and wealth and conquest which appears to shape our human history." No, Jesus' power to vanquish evil is this: "It is the power to heal the wounds which disfigure the image of the Creator in his creatures."

To me, this was the key to the homily—through Jesus, we can be healers by recognizing and tending to the wounds of people we encounter, wounds that obscure the God-granted dignity in each human being.

It reminds me of one of my favorite statements from John Paul, his definition of Christianity as the "deep amazement at man's worth and dignity." This sentence, appearing in Pope John Paul II's first encyclical, *Redemptor Hominis*, amazes me. One would expect a pope to define Christianity in dogmatic terms, as the belief that Jesus is God, the Word, the Second Person of the Trinity. But here, the pope defined Christianity in intensely humanist terms. This deep wonder at others' worth and dignity "is closely connected with Christ," the pope wrote. It is, he wrote, the Good News.

This focus on human dignity is a constant in John Paul's teachings. In his book, *Gift and Mystery*, he explained why: "The two totalitarian systems which tragically marked our century—Nazism on the one hand, marked by the horrors of war and the concentration camps, and communism on the other, with its regime of oppression and terror—I came to know, so to speak, from within. And so it is easy to understand my deep concern for the dignity of every human person and the need to respect human rights, beginning with the right to life. This concern was shaped in the first years of my priesthood and has grown stronger with time."[2]

So often, one hears complaints that organized religion dwells too much on what you shouldn't do. And yes, church leaders can sound so negative as they try to speak out against a wayward culture. They are accused of letting religion "intrude." But the core of John Paul's message is optimism, and that could be no more so than in Bethlehem, source of his hope. "Christ's is the power to transform our weak nature and make us capable, through the grace of the Holy Spirit, of peace with one another and communion with God. . . . This is the message of Bethlehem today and forever," he declared. Amid all the

hopelessness and poverty and unending hatred between occupier and occupied, Pope John Paul II was intensely optimistic
that a Christ-like love could heal the deep wounds he saw
before him in troubled Bethlehem. But to heal the wounds, they
must be seen. In seeing the wounds, we are seeing Christ rise
in the human beings we encounter. And in seeing the risen
Christ, the New Testament tells us in 1 John 3:2, we will see all
we aspire to: "We know that when he [Christ] appears we shall
be like him, for we shall see him as he is."

The Muezzin's Prayer

God is most great. God is most great.
God is most great. God is most great.
I testify there is no god except God.
I testify there is no god except God.
I testify that Muhammad is the messenger of God.
I testify that Muhammad is the messenger of God.
Come to prayer! Come to prayer!
Come to success! Come to success!
God is most great. God is most great.
There is no god except God.

Reflection

As soon as Pope John Paul completed his homily by invoking the Child of Bethlehem and wishing all peace—*"Assalamu
alaikum"*—the loud, lyric Arabic chant of a muezzin calling
Muslims to prayer broke forth from cone-shaped speakers
ringing a minaret that towers above Manger Square. Heard five
times a day, the call to prayer is part of the fabric of everyday
life in the Arab world, a sign of piety well respected by many
Christians, including the pope.

But I must admit that on this occasion, in the midst of a Mass
that marked the heart of John Paul's long-desired pilgrimage,
my first reaction was negative. The pope had just given a stir-

ring homily in the very place where, as he would say, the turning event in human history took place with the birth of Jesus Christ. Couldn't the Muslims, I wondered, give the Catholics a break and delay their midday prayer just this once? Or maybe mute the loudspeakers? This was, after all, a Mass being broadcast around the world.

The Mass became very quiet as the muezzin's voice dominated the square. Notebook in hand, I looked around quickly for signs that a controversy was forming. Some pilgrims looked down nervously, and I heard a tut of resentment from a few. "Even here," someone said. I thought I saw some of the priests seated near the altar tighten in reaction to the intrusion. There was tension.

Religious rivalry among the children of Abraham is, of course, ingrained in the Holy Land, with its awful history of conquerors who wiped out whatever was holy to other faiths. Houses of worship were built over and around those of other faiths. The Mosque of Omar near the Church of the Holy Sepulchre in Jerusalem has two tall minarets, each equidistant from the tomb of Christ inside the church—a visual expression of Muslim teachings overshadowing the Christian belief that Jesus rose from the dead.

To this day, each religion continues to stake its claim against the others (and the Christian churches against one another). This sometimes becomes international news, as with the plan to build a mosque next to the Basilica of the Annunciation in Nazareth. But it's also more subtle. Church bells seem to ring louder in the Holy Land and the muezzin's calls are more amplified. Flags are very prominent, often flying from church spires. That helps delineate each religion's territory, especially in the Old City of Jerusalem. Worship at a holy place is seen as a claim to possession of it.

The call to prayer from the crescent-topped spire of Omar bin al-Kiata Mosque in Bethlehem seemed to fit the pattern, so while I looked closely for reaction, I felt a twinge of resentment. But as I found out later, I couldn't have been more wrong.

Patriarch Michel Sabbah, a bald, white-haired, Nazareth-born Palestinian who heads the Roman Catholic Church in the Holy Land, said something to the congregation in Arabic after the muezzin's call ended and a shout and cheer quickly swelled in Manger Square. Since I don't speak Arabic, I was left to wonder what kind of remark he'd made.

After the Mass ended, I found out the patriarch had explained that church and mosque officials coordinated the call to prayer, which had been delayed to accommodate the pope's homily. "His Holiness gave you his greetings, we said 'amen,' and the muezzin said 'God is most great,' " the patriarch had said in Arabic. "And we witness once again the unity of Muslims and Christians."

For the people gathered there that day—most of them Arab Christians, so used to being a tiny minority—it was a monumental event. From 11:47 a.m. to 11:50 a.m. (four minutes late), the Muslim prayer had mingled with the Mass in an astonishing way. And in his silence, Pope John Paul II had allowed it to happen. He sat quietly in his chair, hands clasped close to his face, and listened. Looking back, it seemed that he'd been savoring the moment thoughtfully.

The pope has always encouraged better relations with Muslims, in the spirit of the Second Vatican Council. In 1985, he addressed 80,000 Muslim youths at a stadium in Casablanca, Morocco, an amazing event. He's praised Muslims for their strong belief in the God of Abraham and for their practice of stopping five times a day to pray. But whenever he's spoken or written about Islam, he's been careful to point out the differences, particularly to affirm Christian belief in the Trinity. And he's been very concerned about fundamentalist Muslim persecution of Christians.

This time, he spoke through his silence.

People were in tears after the Mass. Christians and Muslims get along relatively well in Israel and the West Bank, particularly given their religions' long, bloody history. Still, there are some serious tensions and now, the Christians who took part in the Mass felt liberated from the burden. "I have no words to tell you what my feelings are," said Suad Sfeir, a Christian woman from Bethlehem who finally explained to me what had happened. "I am speechless. I don't know what to say." In addition to the coordinated prayer, she pointed out that during the Mass' kiss of peace, when the congregation is invited to share a sign of Christ's peace, "everybody was greeting the soldiers and they are Muslims."

Her husband Tony, who was born in Bethlehem and whose father received Communion from the pope, explained to me that "both were praising God." He, too, was overcome by this show of unity and hopeful that it would help break down walls.

"It was really . . . " His voice faltered as he put his hand to his heart.

And so the Sfeirs taught me a lesson—about jumping to conclusions, about resentment and, ultimately, about how to be touched by the joy of one of the great moments in Pope John Paul II's pilgrimage to the Holy Land.

Bethlehem: Dheisheh Refugee Camp

The Prayer

Dear refugees, do not think that your present condition makes you any less important in God's eyes! Never forget your dignity as his children! Here at Bethlehem the Divine Child was laid in a manger in a stable; shepherds from the nearby fields were the first to receive the heavenly message of peace and hope for the world. God's design was fulfilled in the

midst of humility and poverty. . . . Dear aid workers
and volunteers, believe in the task you are fulfilling!
Genuine and practical solidarity with those in need
is not a favor conceded, it is a demand of our shared
dignity and a recognition of the dignity of every
human being. Let us all turn with confidence to the
Lord, asking him to inspire those in a position of
responsibility to promote justice, security and peace,
without delay and in an eminently practical way.

The Place

Dheisheh refugee camp, located just outside Bethlehem, dif-
fers vastly from the other stops on Pope John Paul II's pilgrimage. It's not some ancient holy place or official office. It doesn't
have a stadium to be transformed into a temporary house of
worship. Its residents are Muslims. Built on a hill in 1949 to
house Palestinian refugees streaming in from West Jerusalem
and hundreds of small villages destroyed in war, it was at the
end of 1999 "home" to 9,624 people, half of them under 16. The
Catholic bishops of the Latin, Melkite, Syrian, Armenian and
Chaldean rites described it this way in a press release: "In
Dheisheh over an area of a square kilometer are a little less than
650 dwellings on two to three levels, all in miserable conditions. Overcrowded, they have no privacy. The essential services are precarious, starting with hygenic ones, the electricity
is frequently cut and in summer time the water supply is very
scarce. There is no productive activity; unemployment hits
sixty percent of men capable of work. The rest are casual workers in Israel, if they get permission. . . ."

Reflection

If some of the décor surrounding the papal Mass in Manger
Square was insistently political, the trappings awaiting Pope
John Paul II later that afternoon at the Dheisheh refugee camp

were much more so. Slogans were spray-painted on walls: "Who will end 52 years of homelessness?" Children were dressed in T-shirts with the names of Palestinian villages destroyed in 1948. Balloons were also released bearing the villages' names. Murals told the refugees' story and photo displays were devoted to the treatment of Palestinian political prisoners held in Israel. And when the pope spoke from a stage at Dheisheh's School for Boys, he stood beneath a banner declaring "The Right of Return Is a Sacred Right," an attempt to sacralize the Palestinians' long-sought political goal of regaining property the Israelis seized in war. The Palestinians' leader, Yasser Arafat, was buoyant as the pope, arriving in his popemobile, brought the world's attention to Dheisheh. He grabbed hold of church workers in the papal entourage and kissed them.

For many people from Israel and the West, it was a disconcerting sight. Here was John Paul, who had helped in the peaceful toppling of European communism and worked so hard to improve Catholic-Jewish relations, lending his support to a cause they chiefly noticed for terrorist bombings and anti-Semitic rhetoric. Commentators made excuses for him. They blamed the Palestinians for imposing a political overlay on the pope's visit. They implied that John Paul was making a strong gesture to the Palestinians only to be consistent with long-standing Vatican diplomatic policy in the Middle East. Or they said he was not really making a strong gesture at all, that he was merely restating previous church policy and breaking no new ground in Bethlehem. And in the end, there was a chance for those so inclined to turn up their noses at the Palestinians, whose inexperienced police got into a pitched rock-throwing battle with youths at the camp within an hour of the pope's departure from the camp. It was the headline for his stop at Dheisheh.

John Paul's visit to Dheisheh was the most political event of his pilgrimage, no doubt. But even so, he put the refugees' struggles into a larger religious and cultural context, with much more powerful results than if he had commented directly on such issues of the day as Palestinian statehood. Immediately, he put the visit into a religious context: "It is important to me that my pilgrimage to the birthplace of Jesus Christ, on this two thousandth anniversary of that extraordinary event, includes this visit to Dheishch," he told the refugees and relief workers. "It is deeply significant that here, close to Bethlehem, I am meeting you. . . . Throughout my pontificate I have felt close to the Palestinian people in their sufferings."

Why was it so important? The birth of Jesus brought God into the world in Bethlehem so that he could show us how to be truly human—by being loving, as God is. Every person deserves to be treated with the dignity inherent in a creature made in God's image, but that wasn't so for the refugees, whom he told: "You have been deprived of many things which represent basic needs of the human person: proper housing, health care, education and work."

But there was something even worse than material deprivation, and it is here that the pope touched on one of the great themes of his life. *"Above all,"* he told these long-term refugees, "you bear the sad memory of what you were forced to leave behind. Not just material possessions, but your freedom, the closeness of relatives, and the familiar surroundings and cultural traditions which nourished your personal and family life."

As a young man, Karol Wojtyla was a refugee. With his father, he fled the oncoming Nazi invasion of Poland, only to turn back as the Soviet army advanced from the east. He knew what it was like to live under occupation —and not by a democratic government like Israel, but by the amoral, genocidal Nazis. Just as his literary and acting talent was beginning to bloom, Wojtyla found himself living in a slave state that sought absolute control over its subjects. To that end, the Nazis tried to wipe out Polish culture, to kill all traces of freedom. Schools were shut. Participation in cultural activities was a capital offense. Libraries were demolished. Theaters were closed, open only to Germans. The statue of a revered national poet, Adam Mickiewicz, was destroyed in the center of Kraków's Old Town. It was against the law to play Chopin.[3]

"Every vestige of Polish culture is to be eliminated,"[4] declared the Nazis' vicious henchman in Poland, Hans Frank.

During those years, in which he worked as a laborer in a quarry and a chemical plant, the pope-to-be studied secretly in clandestine classes at Jagiellonian University, which the Nazis had closed. Then he secretly became a seminarian. As if that risk weren't enough at a time when thousands of priests and sisters were being executed (because of the Church's key role in Polish culture), he took part in a surprisingly active but secret theater troupe—a deliberate effort to flout the Nazi attempt to eliminate Polish culture.

So John Paul's sympathy for the Palestinian refugees' loss of "freedom, the closeness of relatives, and the familiar surroundings and cultural traditions which nourished your personal and family life" is deeply rooted in his own life. When he says he appreciates the Palestinians' suffering, he means it.

John Paul's experience with Polish defiance of the Nazis and later, the Soviets, showed him that culture was a powerful enough force to undermine even the most fearsome governments. Every nation, he told the United Nations General Assembly in 1995, "enjoys the right to its own language and culture. . . . History shows that in extreme circumstances (such as those which occurred in the land where I was born) it is precisely its culture that enables a nation to survive the loss of political and economic independence."

And so the question of whether a nation—a people—achieves statehood, as the Palestinians so desire, is not quite so important to John Paul as the health and freedom of its cultural traditions. For, as he said at the UN, "The heart of every culture is its approach to the greatest of all mysteries: the mystery of God." Or, as author George Weigel put it, "He was convinced that culture drove history, over the long run...and the most powerful component of culture was cult, or religion."[5]

John Paul had come to encourage the Palestinian refugees, to show them their own dignity as children of Bethlehem, to "bring some comfort in your difficult situation." He had granted a worldwide stage to their hopes, to their murals, banners, folk dances and political graffiti, a bowl of their soil, their T-shirts and photos, and even to their heavy-handed political leaders—in short, to their national culture. "Please God, it will help to draw attention to your continuing plight," he said of his visit.

Worse than their poverty—the refugees are assisted by the UN and relief organizations such as the papal charity Catholic Near East Welfare Association—was their anger, their hopelessness, their wounded longing for homes lost a half-century ago, their sense of alienation at being separated from families and their villages, which are so important in Middle East culture. "Do not think that your present condition makes you any less important in God's eyes!" John Paul told them. "Never forget your dignity as his children!"

In his travels, John Paul likes to draw out the best in the cultures he encounters. I saw this on his visit to New York, Newark and Baltimore in 1995, when he spoke of how Americans' prized freedoms were rooted in their founding fathers' religiously based moral principles. "Do not be afraid to search for God," he said in a Mass in New York's Central Park. "Then it will truly be the land of the free and the home of the brave."

At Dheisheh, he also reached into the past to encourage the people he was visiting. After describing how Jesus was born in Bethlehem "in the midst of humility and poverty," he looked up from his prepared text and inserted an ad-lib: "Probably, the shepherds of Bethlehem were your predecessors, your ancestors." Judging from the applause from the camp's residents, who were Muslims, it was the best thing the pope said all that day to the Palestinian people. Arafat looked especially gleeful, perhaps because it fed into the politicized argument which surrounds his claim that the thoroughly Jewish Jesus was a Palestinian. More to the point, though, I think the pope had struck a chord because he was viewing the Palestinians in the way they see themselves but the world does not—as a simple, pastoral people, close to the land, close to God, and hospitable to all, even to a baby whose first crib was a feeding trough. One must hope that such a peaceful image, drawn from the Gospel of Luke, will play some small role in helping the Palestinians to overcome the extremist political parties within their own ranks, reject violence and risk peace. The shepherds of Bethlehem, as the pope said, were "the first to receive the heavenly message of peace and hope for the world." The Palestinians, he implied, must see themselves as heirs to that legacy.

But they cannot be expected to make this venture alone, the pope indicated, declaring that Palestinians' rights would continue to be violated until political leaders acted in "solidarity" to serve the common good. Solidarity, the pope has written elsewhere, comes about when people "recognize one another as persons"—that is, see each other's wounds. *"Opus solidaritatis pax,"* John Paul has written. "Peace as the fruit of solidarity."[6]

No, Pope John Paul II did not endorse creation of an independent Palestinian state that day, despite some news reports that said so. Instead, he declared that the Palestinians' God-given rights as a people were being violated before the world and would remain so until political leaders learned to see past narrow self-interest.

Powerful words—and a lesson that the Christian duty to love one's neighbor and recognize the dignity of individuals extends even to entire nations, in this case the Palestinian people.

Questions for Reflection

1. Can you think of times when you saw someone's hidden wounds, "the wounds which disfigure the image of the Creator in his creatures"? What did you do or could you have done to respond? Is it possible to see the wounds of an entire nation? If so, give an example.

2. What does it mean to you when Pope John Paul II speaks of the "eternal today of God's salvation"?

3. Have you seen times when people respond too harshly to what they perceive as slights against their religion? What is your reaction?

4. What is your reaction to the kind words Pope John Paul II had for Palestinians in his trip to Bethlehem and the Dheisheh refugee camp?

5. Pope John Paul II managed to speak out in the Palestinians' behalf without alienating his friends in Israel. Why did that happen? And what model does it offer for speaking out on controversial justice issues without rancor?

6. How important a role does religion have in the culture of your community?

Chapter 4

Jerusalem: The Cenacle

The trip's busy fourth day started with a private Mass in the Upper Room that is the traditional site of Jesus' Last Supper, on what is now known as Mount Zion in Jerusalem. An elevator installed especially for the event brought the pope up to the room, which is also the traditional site of Pentecost. Later, John Paul held two meetings that helped cement Vatican relations with Israel: first, a private session with Chief Ashkenazic Rabbi Israel Meir Lau and Chief Sephardic Rabbi Eliyahu Bakshi-Doron at Heichal Shlomo in Jerusalem, the seat of the Israeli chief rabbinate, followed by a meeting with Israeli President Ezer Weizman at his residence. Then John Paul went to the Israeli Holocaust memorial in Jerusalem, Yad Vashem, and finally, to a late-afternoon interreligious ceremony. In this chapter, Bob wrote about the Cenacle, Paul the physical description of Yad Vashem and the first reflection on Yad Vashem, Bob the second reflection on Yad Vashem, and Paul the section on the interreligious ceremony.

The Prayer

In the Incarnation, the Son of God, of one being with the Father, became Man and received a body from the Virgin Mary. And now, on the night before his death, he says to his disciples: "This is my Body, which will be given up for you."

It is with deep emotion that we listen once more to these words spoken here in this Upper Room two thousand years ago. Since then they have been repeated, generation after generation, by those who share in the priesthood of Christ through the Sacrament of Holy Orders. In this way, Christ himself constantly says these words anew, through the voice of his priests in every corner of the world.

The Place

On our second day in Jerusalem, well before the pope arrived, Paul and I had prayed at the Western Wall, then walked toward the Zion Gate at the southern end of the Old City. There, after a series of twists and turns and stairways, we somehow found the Cocnaculum, the Cenacle, located together in the same building as the traditional Tomb of King David.

The conjunction of these two sites so close together is typical of Jerusalem. Around every corner is something that almost forces pilgrims to stop, think, and pray. Between the Cenacle and the Old City's wall, for example, is the Abbey of the Dormition, where we attended evening prayer a few minutes after our brief stop at the Cenacle. Though the monks chanted entirely in German, I found this stop meaningful, because this abbey gave birth to Weston Priory in Vermont, whose music has been an important part of my own spirituality for decades. A little beyond the Cenacle, to the south of the walls, is the grave of Oskar Schindler, who saved from the Nazis more than 1,000 Jews in Kraków, the ancient city where the pope survived the occupation and later in his life became archbishop.

In the middle of all this, we found a few minutes to stand in the Cenacle and try to reflect on the Last Supper. But I must admit, to my untrained eye, the Cenacle did not appear like an upper room from the time of Jesus. The building's current shape dates to the fourteenth century, and the Gothic arches give the room a medieval ambience. "The tradition concerning this building as the site of the Last Supper is unreliable," writes Father Jerome Murphy-O'Connor, one of the most respected experts on biblical sites in the Holy Land. The first testimony about this site dates to the fifth century, he explains, apparently derived from "the better supported tradition which located on Mount Sion the descent of the Spirit on the apostles at Pentecost."[1] Still, tradition is a powerful thing, and this room has for centuries been associated with the Last Supper, with the first Eucharist, with the creation of the sacramental priesthood, with the Spirit's inspiration of the early church. And it is likely that those events did occur somewhere close to this site. So it was irresistible to John Paul, a priest for more than half a century. If he had not chosen to celebrate Mass here, it would have been a major upset. In fact, despite the archaeological skepticism about its authenticity as the exact site of the Last Supper, one church official said that this room was one of the pope's favorite places on the pilgrimage.

Reflection

This pope is the most productive writer ever to sit in the Chair of Peter. The astonishing volume of his writing reminds me of Thomas Merton, one of my great heroes. Of course, style is another matter. Merton wrote like an angel, in sharp, well-aimed sentences, crafted from acutely sensory images, and launched with an unerring sense of trajectory. John Paul writes like a philosopher-pope, too often marching his thoughts across the page as naked ideas, chilled and shivering without personal words, the warm flesh and blood that make sentences come alive.

In sharp contrast to the dense style of his most abstract writing, perhaps John Paul's most readable and human work was his 1996 book, *Gift and Mystery,* published at the fiftieth anniversary of his priesthood. It glowed with humanity, telling real stories about his own life and offering sharp insights into priesthood, not as a theological abstraction, but as a vivid reality lived by a man named Karol Wojtyla, a strong man who overcame loneliness, tragedy and the oppression of two crushing tyrannies to embrace the priestly life. When he marked the golden jubilee of his ordination, he invited priests from all over the world to join him in Rome and celebrate joyfully with him their common gift and mystery.

In the context of five decades as a priest, John Paul under-
standably saw his private Mass at the Cenacle as a glowing
moment. "Our priesthood was born in the Upper Room
together with the Eucharist," he wrote in his annual Holy
Thursday letter to priests, which he signed during the visit to
the Cenacle. Considering the significance of the event and the
intense emotion that it appeared to elicit among those present
in the room, however, I found the pope's homily here a bit flat,
too much of the philosopher-pope, and not enough of the very
human pope of *Gift and Mystery*. In contrast, the letter to priests
offered more down-to-earth touches, such as his meditation on
the Last Supper.

"Spiritually, I see Jesus and the Apostles seated at table with
him," John Paul wrote. "I think of Peter especially: it is as if I
can see him, with the other disciples, watching in amazement
the Lord's actions, listening with deep emotion to his words
and, for all the burden of his frailty, opening himself to the
mystery proclaimed here and soon to be accomplished." He
reflects on the contrast between the complete self-giving that
Jesus offered in the Eucharist and the evil that Judas chose. And
he points out that the author of the Gospel of John does not
mention the institution of the Eucharist, but does include the
story of the washing of the feet. "Even more than an example
of humility offered for our imitation, this action of Jesus, so disconcerting to Peter, is a revelation of the radicalness of God's
condescension toward us," John Paul wrote.

Here, condescension does not carry the secondary meaning
of "patronizing attitude or behavior," but the primary one, "a
voluntary descent from one's rank or dignity in relations with
an inferior."[2] John Paul cites the great Christological hymn
quoted by Paul in his letter to the Philippians. This passage,
perhaps my favorite in all of Scripture, was the early Church's
lyrical celebration of the way Jesus "emptied himself, taking
the form of a slave, being born in human likeness."[3] The fancy
Greek term for this radical self-emptying is *kenosis*. In Greek or

in English, this reality is central to any understanding of Jesus. He expressed this self-emptying most definitively at the Crucifixion itself, but in a less agonizing, more embraceable way, he displayed it in the Upper Room (wherever the actual room was), in the washing of the feet. Gregory Norbet, who wrote so much of the music of Weston Priory, captured this moment musically in the refrain of one of my favorite hymns: "The Lord Jesus, after eating with his friends, washed their feet and said to them: Do you know what I, your Lord, have done to you? I have given you example, that so you also should do."[4]

In his letter to priests, John Paul reached out to them in a personal way: "In this holy room I naturally find myself imagining you in all the various parts of the world, with your myriad faces, some younger, some more advanced in years, in all the different emotional states which you are experiencing: for many, thank God, joy and enthusiasm, for others perhaps suffering or weariness or discouragement." He's right. I know my share of priests who still bring immense joy and enthusiasm to their work, even as the demands of their life become more difficult. With the number of priests dwindling and the number of Catholics increasing, the remaining priests feel rising levels of stress. Sadly, too many have decided not to remain, because of the growing workload, or clashes with the hierarchy, and sometimes because they find they can no longer give to the Church the priceless but difficult gift of celibacy. Among many who have left the active priesthood and married, the call to ministry is still powerful.

From the global perspective of Rome, the problem can look smaller than it does from the pews. In many parts of the world, the Vatican reasons, increasing numbers of young men are entering seminaries to study for the priesthood. But in those parts of the world where that is not true, such as large regions of the United States, the blooming of vocations in another place does not offer much of a consolation. One example is the Diocese of Brooklyn, where I grew up and briefly studied for the priesthood myself. In July 2000, a few months after the pope's Mass at the Cenacle, Bishop Thomas Daily issued a pastoral letter, *Pray the Lord of the Harvest*, about the dwindling numbers of priests in his diocese. The problem has reached "urgent and serious" proportions, Bishop Daily wrote. Later, some bishops told him privately that he had done them a favor by writing so publicly about an issue that had troubled other regions in the United States long before it reached a "sobering" stage in his diocese. They also told him that a pastoral letter from a bishop in the populous Northeast might help get the Vatican's attention.

The core of the issue is the availability of the Eucharist. Though John Paul did not address the availability question, the Eucharist itself was obviously a central theme of his homily at the Cenacle. "Through the Eucharist, Christ builds up the Church," he said. "Through the celebration of the Eucharist, he never ceases to draw men and women to be effective members of his Body."

Since the Eucharist is the center of Catholic faith, and priesthood is essential to the celebration of the Eucharist, all Catholics should "pray the Lord of the harvest" that the Spirit will lead us to solve the problem of declining numbers of priests—through increasingly effective recruitment of new vocations or whatever other steps the Spirit leads us to choose. It would be wonderful if, on some future visit to the Cenacle, John Paul or one of his successors could sign a Holy Thursday letter to priests that would rejoice over the solution. That is profoundly to be hoped.

Jerusalem: Yad Vashem

The Prayer

In this place of solemn remembrance, I fervently pray that our sorrow for the tragedy which the

Jewish people suffered in the twentieth century will lead to a new relationship between Christians and Jews. Let us build a new future in which there will be no more anti-Jewish feelings among Christians and anti-Christian feeling among Jews, but rather the mutual respect required of those who adore the one Creator and Lord, and look to Abraham as our common father in faith.

The world must heed the warning that comes to us from the victims of the Holocaust and from the testimony of the survivors. Here at Yad Vashem the memory lives on, and burns itself into our souls. It makes us cry out:

I hear the whispering of many – terror on every side! But I trust in you O Lord: I say You are my God. *(Psalm 31:13-15)*

The Place

Yad Vashem is Israel's memorial to the six million Jews killed in the *Shoah*—its name, which means "a memorial and a name," comes from Isaiah 56:5: "I will give, in my house and within my walls, a monument and a name better than sons and daughters; I will give them an everlasting name that shall not be cut off." Built on a hauntingly quiet, wooded, 45-acre hillside site in West Jerusalem, it includes museums; a research library; the tree-lined Avenue of the Righteous, a walkway dedicated to those who risked their lives to save Jews from the Nazis; a memorial to the 1.5 million children killed in the Holocaust and the Hall of Remembrance. We visited several days before the pope's arrival and, like everyone else who goes there, could not fail to be deeply affected. First we walked among the pines and cypress trees lining the Avenue of the Righteous, where plaques honor the gentiles who risked their lives to save Jews from the Nazis, people like Oskar and Emilie Schindler. (The majority of these trees honor Polish Catholics.)

Then we entered the Hall of Remembrance, which the pope was to visit. With its walls made of huge boulders and its concrete ceiling pitched upward at an angle, the Hall of Remembrance is stark, foreboding and, as its name implies, evocative. A flame lights the darkness, giving off smoke that rises up slowly and exits through a small square at the roof's apex, like an eternally renewed sacrifice. The nearby historical museum is powerful in its own way, a collection of photos and other exhibits that shows how the Nazis first set out to humiliate the Jews through discriminatory laws, then restricted them to ghettos and finally moved to mass murder. It underscores the need to be vigilant about infringements on civil liberties. Since we both covered the pope's visit to Yad Vashem for *Newsday*, we've each written a reflection here—Paul on the official ceremony and Bob on the reaction of Israeli Holocaust survivors who watched on television.

Paul's Reflection

When I was 6 or 7 years old, I was astonished to find a box of small, very old-looking orange candles as I rummaged through a cabinet in my grandparents' home in search of a game, a version of Chinese checkers. I immediately recognized them as Chanukah candles, although more old-fashioned than the orange bulbs typically seen on menorahs in my Brooklyn neighborhood.

"Grandma," I asked. "What *are* these?"

I'd never seen a menorah in my grandparents' attached brick home in the Bay Ridge neighborhood of Brooklyn. Nor had I seen any other sign that my grandparents, Dr. Samuel Moses and his wife, Minna Moses, were Jewish. There had never been any reason to believe they were anything other than Catholic, like myself and almost everyone else in the world I knew.

My grandmother explained to me that these were in fact Hanukkah candles. So I asked: "Grandma, are you *Jewish*?"

And then I put those candles back into the cabinet—a cabinet, I now know, that was among the few belongings my grandparents were able to save when they left their home in Germany in 1938 and fled from the Nazis.

In covering Pope John Paul II's trip to the Holy Land, I found that personal stories about how the Holocaust touched individual people were everywhere to be found. Whether it was the top officials of the Israeli government, the leading rabbis or the man or woman in the street, a discussion of the Holocaust almost always turned to the personal, to the family history. It is probably the only way to comprehend the immensity of the event.

The pope connected in this way, too. When he visited the Hall of Remembrance at Yad Vashem, he did not deliver some long, weighty treatise. Instead, his remarks were brief and pastoral. He communicated far more in his silence and in the consoling gestures he shared with Holocaust survivors who gathered to witness his visit. He connected one-to-one with people like Edith Tzirer, a 69-year-old woman who recalls that a young Karol Wojtyla found her in a train station after her release from a Nazi labor camp, too weak with tuberculosis to walk. She said he had given her bread and hot tea, then carried the 13-year-old girl two miles on his back to an orphanage. Tzirer wept as she greeted this man, now aged and clothed in the white papal robes, during the ceremony at Yad Vashem. The pope lingered with her, rubbing her shoulder as she cried. After the ceremony, he met again with the Holocaust survivors and their families, many of them from his hometown of Wadowice—"an extraordinarily moving moment for him," a Vatican official later said.

My own family's story weighed heavily on my mind as I covered these emotional events, which showed how the ground underlying Jewish-Catholic relations has indeed shifted in my lifetime.

As a boy, the idea that I was half-Jewish was very difficult to accept, since I grew up in a thoroughly Catholic setting. Both of my parents were churchgoing Catholics; so was almost everyone else on my block. At Mary Queen of Heaven School in Brooklyn's Flatlands section, my arithmetic workbook had addition exercises in which I tallied pictures of rosaries and other religious items. In history class, the stories of saints tortured by the Indians were told in great detail. As an altar boy, I memorized the Latin Mass. And as I remember catechism class, we were taught that only Catholics could go to heaven. Others would, at best, wind up in limbo.

It was my fervent hope that someday I could manage a deathbed baptism of my grandparents—we were instructed on how to do emergency baptisms. That would have been a twist on what is now probably a quiet trend in which devout grandparents secretly baptize their infant grandchildren, a few drops of water and a heartfelt prayer when the parents are out at the movies.

Over the years, I learned bits and pieces of my family's story. My grandfather had been a prominent doctor in Lorrach, Germany, a town at the southwestern corner of the country near the Swiss and French borders. In 1938, my grandparents and their two sons, including my father, Bernard, fled to Switzerland and then made their way to Brooklyn, where my grandfather passed the medical examination in English and started a new practice. During his military service in World War II, my father converted to Roman Catholicism. A religious man, he was seeking something he hadn't found in his non-observant family. My grandfather's acceptance of this was symbolized by his annual gift to my father of the Jesuit magazine *America,* and one of my proudest days as a writer occurred when I was able to call my father and tell him I had an article in the magazine.

For years, I would not admit the obvious to my friends, that I was half Jewish. I was, though, sensitive to the anti-Semitism that seemed to pervade my growing years. I can remember the swastikas, crosses and the phrase "Christ killers" painted in graffiti on the outside of Rose's candy store. Today, there are rightfully stories in the newspaper when swastikas are painted. Back then, in the early 1960s, it wasn't news, I guess.

I took a great deal of teasing about my last name, Moses. When asked, I insisted I was German, not Jewish. But perhaps it was not so far off, since my grandparents seemed to have a German household. Sauerbraten and red cabbage were the special dishes; for lunch, there were sausages from the German butcher. My grandfather had served on the front in World War I as a doctor, and had a picture of himself in that bleak landscape. His father had fought in the Franco-Prussian War. When my father was a boy in Germany, he had blond hair with his blue eyes, most handsome. He sometimes told the story of a teacher who was expounding to the class on the glories of the Aryan race and hovered over my father, citing him as an example of this Aryan superiority. The rest of the class, knowing that my father was Jewish, laughed.

For the most part, my grandparents and father spoke little of all this. Eventually, I was told that my grandfather's sister, Regina, had perished in the Holocaust. She lived in Holland, where she had gone after marrying, and was later sent to Auschwitz. When my daughter Caitlin was born in 1983, we gave her Regina as a middle name. And when I visited Auschwitz on a reporting assignment in 1987, I prayed for her and wrote a note to her in the visitors' book. It was a jarring experience to visit that death camp, but in some ways I was still like the taxi driver who took me there from nearby Kraków. All his life, he had been driving visitors to the concentration camp, but he had not once entered it. He could not stare so much death in the face.

The curiosity I had was even stronger in my children. And just a week before I departed for Israel to cover John Paul's pilgrimage, my son Matthew, then 20, opened a door to the past. Matthew, on recess from his college studies in Florence, traveled through northern Europe and stopped in my father's hometown. The only information he had was my father's old address, 6 Wilhelmstrasse. But the street, named after Kaiser Wilhelm, Germany's emperor during World War I, didn't exist. So he went to the town hall, presenting the officials there with a young life that would never have existed had the Nazis succeeded. He was received graciously and, in short order, a detailed file about the Moses family was produced from the basement archives. The clerk pulled out a biography of my grandfather, newspaper clippings, information on relatives I'd never heard of, a history of the Jewish community of Lorrach complete with a map showing where the Moses family sat in the synagogue—even the deed to the house, which was transferred to a family whose name Matthew found was still on the doorbell.

This was the backdrop for my visit with Bob to Yad Vashem several days before the pope's arrival. Bob was really my guide; he knew far more about the Holocaust than I did. When we entered the darkened Hall of Remembrance, wearing yarmulkes, as required, he pointed to the names of the camps etched into the floor, surrounding an eternal flame. One of them was Westerbork. Bob explained that it was a transit point for Dutch Jews, and that my great-aunt Regina would have been brought there before being sent to Auschwitz.

The prayer of John Paul I'll remember most at that location was his silent gaze at the eternal flame, which he re-lit. Light from the flames glowed on his face, this face of a man who had struggled to reshape the twentieth century for the good, this face of a man who had witnessed the depth of its horrors in the Poland of the Second World War. I thought of Isaiah—"I set my face like flint." Unlike my cab driver in Kraków, John Paul was not afraid to be touched by the memory of the Holocaust's horrors. In fact, when John Paul visited Auschwitz in 1979, he said it was "impossible for me not to come here as pope." There was a rock-hard strength in the pope's face as the memories screamed past him in the silence. He thought, no doubt, of some of the Polish Jews he counted as friends during his years growing up in Wadowice.

In his address at Yad Vashem, the pope wisely leaned on the Book of Psalms. It condenses into poetry the history of the Jewish people, their liberation in Egypt, their struggles with invaders, their depths and their hope and joy in God—a perfect choice for a place that sanctifies the memory of the Holocaust. Those who pray the psalms can join the psalmist in expressing the deepest human emotions—hatred, anger, desolation, forgiveness, joy, love, among others—which find their place in this amazing prayer book. It encompasses even the incomprehensible, the *Shoah*. And it gives prayerful expression to anger against God.

The Pope started his remarks by quoting Psalm 31:

I have become like a broken vessel,

I hear the whispering of many—terror on every side—as they scheme together against me, as they plot to take my life.

But I trust in you, O Lord; I say, "You are my God."

To experience Yad Vashem—or for that matter, to empathize with suffering of any kind—is to "become like a broken vessel," to hear "the whispering of many," to sense the "terror on every side." John Paul spoke then of his most intense prayer at Yad Vashem, his silence. "In this place of memories, the mind and heart and soul feel an extreme need for silence. Silence in which to remember. Silence in which to try to make some sense of the memories, which come flooding back. Silence because there are no words strong enough to deplore the terrible tragedy of the *Shoah*."

Much has been written about what John Paul said in his visit to the Holy Land, but little about what perhaps mattered most to him—the silence. And yet there is an "extreme need" for silence. It is the way to remember. He indicated that such memories weighed on his own mind: "My own personal memories are of all that happened when the Nazis occupied Poland during the War. I remember my Jewish friends and neighbors, some of whom perished, while others survived."

His remarks reminded me of a meeting I'd been at several days earlier with a group of visiting reporters and Jerusalem's chief Ashkenazic rabbi, Israel Meir Lau. When the rabbi greeted us in a meeting room near his office, it struck me that he resembled my grandfather. Odd, I know, because my grandfather was secular, non-observant, clean-shaven but for a mustache. But they both seemed to have a certain upright bearing that commanded respect, perhaps some physical resemblance, and were both very learned. And Rabbi Lau proceeded to tell a story about his own grandfather.

"The pope knew even my grandfather from the city of Kraków," the rabbi said, recalling that John Paul remembered his grandfather walking to synagogue, surrounded by children.

"How many grandchildren did he have?" John Paul asked.

"Forty-seven," the rabbi told him.

"And how many survived?" he asked.

"Five survived," the chief rabbi answered.

At that, the rabbi said, John Paul looked at the ceiling, then spoke of the importance to him that all be "committed to the future and the continuity of our senior brother, the Jewish community."

The lesson was clear for Rabbi Lau. "He experienced Jewish suffering," the rabbi said.

John Paul came not only as the leader of a great religion—he came as a man who wanted to remember people he had known. He came, too, to see the wounds of the Jewish people, just as he had seen the Palestinians' wounds in his visit to the refugee camp. For to love someone, to see someone as a sibling, is to see his or her wounds without turning away. "I have come to Yad Vashem to pay homage to the millions of Jewish people who, stripped of everything, especially of their human dignity, were murdered in the Holocaust," he said. "More than half a century has passed, but the memories remain."

Here too, John Paul returned to his focus on human dignity rooted in humankind's creation in God's image. To be Christian is to be amazed at the God-given dignity of every human being and to hear the laments of those whose dignity is denied. "Here, as at Auschwitz and many other places in Europe, we are overcome by the echo of the heart-rending laments of so many," he said. "Men, women and children cry out to us from the depths of the horror that they knew. How can we fail to heed their cry?"

To deny human dignity is to deny God. "How could man have such utter contempt for man?" John Paul asked. "Because he had reached the point of contempt for God. Only a Godless ideology could plan and carry out the extermination of a whole people."

The optimism of John Paul's Christian humanism shone through even in this dark and somber setting. He referred to the Avenue of the Righteous and gentiles who gave their lives to save Jews, saying, "That is why the Psalms, and the entire Bible, though aware of the human capacity for evil, also proclaim that evil will not have the last word."

For news purposes, the most closely watched aspect of John Paul's speech was whether or not he would specifically address the Catholic Church's actions during the Holocaust. He did not issue the apology many Israelis had hoped for, saying instead:

"As Bishop of Rome and Successor of the Apostle Peter, I assure the Jewish people that the Catholic Church, motivated by the Gospel law of truth and love and by no political considerations, is deeply saddened by the hatred, acts of persecution and displays of anti-Semitism directed against the Jews by Christians at any time and in any places. The Church rejects racism in any form as a denial of the image of the Creator inherent in every human being."

The statement quotes almost exactly the words of the Second Vatican Council's document *Nostra Aetate*, which was issued in 1965 and opened a new era in Jewish-Catholic relations. John Paul had quoted the same statement when he visited a synagogue in Rome in 1986. It states: "Moreover, mindful of her common patrimony with the Jews, and motivated by the gospel's spiritual love and by no political considerations, she deplores the hatred, persecutions, and displays of anti-Semitism directed against the Jews at any time and from any source."[5] One key difference is that while the council fathers said the church "deplores" persecution of the Jews, John Paul said it is "deeply saddened," a shift from externalized condemnation to a grieving, internalized lament.

It was, though, not what Israelis were hoping for: "Pope falls short of *Shoah* apology" was the headline in the next day's *Jerusalem Post*. And yet, John Paul's visit to Yad Vashem was widely embraced in Israel, with few leaders in its civic, religious or academic communities criticizing him for falling short of Israelis' expectations. John Paul had been quietly working throughout his pontificate to improve his Church's relations with Jews and the Jewish state, an effort most Israelis did not know much about. Israelis involved in interreligious dialogue were still trying to explain to their fellow citizens the significance of decisions the Catholic Church had made 35 years earlier at Vatican II. But now, it had all been summed up in the singular image of having a pope visit Yad Vashem and mourn the six million Jews killed in the Holocaust—some of whom he counted as friends. By the time the pope signaled the end of his remarks by saying, "I fervently pray," there was no doubting his fervor. When he prayed for "a new relationship between Christians and Jews," he was not just being politic. He had come to Yad Vashem to remember, and he did.

But memory is not meant to be an old scrapbook to be pulled out in a sad or nostalgic moment. It demands, right now, that "those who adore the one Creator and Lord" respect each other. And it calls for us to "pray for peace and justice, and to commit ourselves to their cause," John Paul said.

A few weeks after I returned to Brooklyn, my son Matthew's studies in Italy ended and he arrived back home along with the packet of documents he'd gotten in Germany. I was so eager to find out what they said that I quickly typed some of the German documents into my computer's word processor and transferred them to a translation program on the Internet, but the result was still a garble. Soon after, though, my father visited, sat at the dining room table and translated for us.

There was a biography that told of how my grandfather had founded a home for orphans after World War I, devastating years in Germany. When it expanded into a larger building, the town took it over and he remained as medical director. The biography reprinted the letter he received in 1933 when, after the Nazis took control, Jews were no longer permitted to serve as doctors. He was thanked for his services and dismissed from the home he had started. The floor plans for his house were there, and the doctor's office was on the first floor, much as it was when he lived in Brooklyn. A newspaper ad gave his office hours, which were almost identical to those he kept in Brooklyn.

There was an unexpected detail—a second sister, Rosa, was "murdered in Auschwitz," the biography said. I'd never heard of her. There was information on other relatives I'd never heard about, leaving the presumption that they also died in the Holocaust. And I wondered, as the pope had asked of Rabbi Lau, how many more of my grandparents' friends and relatives were murdered.

The biography had a picture of my grandparents as I remembered them, with a doleful look on their faces. It struck me when I saw it that they did not smile in any of their photos. I'd never realized it, but looking back, I could see now that there was a sadness about them, particularly my grandfather. When I was young, it seemed natural to me for them to be sad and a little wistful because they were old. I know better now.

They, too, remembered.

Bob's Reflection

For two decades, as I covered local and state politics for *Newsday*, my work had never presented me an occasion to focus on the Holocaust. Nor had I devoted much of my leisure time to reading or thinking about it.

Then, on a long business trip to northern New York in 1991, I listened to an audio version of *The Diary of Anne Frank*, to help me overcome drowsiness on the road. That brave little book not only kept me from falling asleep at the wheel, but also began awakening me to the reality of "The Final Solution."

Jolted belatedly into sustained thinking and reading on the great evil of anti-Semitism and the monstrous fruit that it bore in the Third Reich, I began to make up for lost time, becoming almost obsessed with the subject.

Late in 1992, I listened to an unabridged audio version of Thomas Keneally's book, *Schindler's List*. I vividly recall arriving at work one morning, with tears in my eyes, as the narrator read its last words. Of all the books I had ever read, I thought, this was the one that I most wished I had written.

A few minutes later, in the office, I searched for anything I could find on the author. A tiny wire-service story told me that Steven Spielberg was planning to make a film based on Keneally's book. Right then, I resolved to find time to report and write a piece about the origins of Keneally's work and how it had seized the imagination of Steven Spielberg, previously known primarily for escapist adventure films.

One of the first people I interviewed was a man who played a key role in Oskar Schindler's efforts to save Jews in wartime Kraków. After the war, Leopold Pfefferberg immigrated to the United States and changed his name to Page, on the advice of an immigration official. He opened a leather goods store in Beverly Hills, where he spent much of his spare time trying to get someone to write Schindler's story. One day, Keneally came to town for a book signing, happened to stop into Page's store to buy a briefcase, listened to Page's urgent retelling of the Schindler story, and agreed to write a book.

Working on that story brought me in contact with other *Schindlerjuden* (Schindler Jews), providing me with my first experiences interviewing survivors. It also connected me by phone with Spielberg, who told me the story of learning his arithmetic at his grandparents' home in Cincinnati by examining the numbers tattooed on a survivor's arm.

The Schindler story appeared in February 1993, just before Spielberg began filming *Schindler's List*. Soon after that, I wrote another Nazi-related story, about a group of college students called the White Rose, who mounted a leafletting campaign against Hitler, protesting the mass extermination of the Jews. The Nazis caught and executed them. Today, dozens of German schools are named for them.

I wrote those first two Holocaust-related stories in the time that I managed to set aside from the long-term projects reporting that was then my assignment. But soon after they appeared, I became a religion writer. Given latitude to define this new beat for myself, I defined it to include the Holocaust.

Since then, I have written often on this compelling subject: about the survivors, about the rescuers, about those who would deny that the murder of European Jewry even happened, about the controversy over the role of Pope Pius XII.

In reporting those stories, I have often sat with survivors, trying to remain gentle enough to honor their suffering, but persistent enough to draw their story forth.

For many, giving voice to the unspeakable, even to tell their own children, had been impossible for decades. Then, as they grew old, they realized that mortality was bringing to an end their chance to testify. Finally, the words tumbled out, haltingly at times and torrentially at others, as a profound sense of duty impelled them to try describing an indescribable evil.

Given that experience, it seemed likely to me that the pope's visit to Yad Vashem would be a crucial moment in his pilgrimage. That's why Paul and I took a cab out to Yad Vashem the Friday morning before the pope was to arrive, to gain a sense of this place that has become so central in the life of the Jewish people. I felt the need for silent reflection as we walked the Avenue of the Righteous and I paused before the tree dedicated to Oskar Schindler.

Writing about Schindler and talking to those who knew him well, I had come to something of an understanding of him. Schindler was a flawed man who profited from the Nazi program of Aryanizing Jewish-owned businesses and residences, but then he had gradually begun to recognize the evil of the Final Solution. Ultimately, he reacted to that great evil with unprecedented generosity and bravery, defying the Nazis and saving more than a thousand Jewish lives. It meant a lot to me to be able to stand before his tree and remember.

In my own life, writing about the Holocaust has given me a painfully detailed understanding of the role of Christians in the Holocaust. It was Christians who, badly misreading the Gospel and falling far short of the teachings of Jesus, had created over the centuries a permanent hell for Jews. For hundreds of years, the Jewish people had suffered from anti-Jewish attitudes and laws. Some popes took steps to mitigate these laws, but others condoned them. They had lived through bloody pogroms, planned and executed by Christians. No wonder that, for them, the Christian symbol of redemption and radical self-giving, the crucifix, had become a hated reminder of persecution.

This long history of anti-Judaism, a nasty thread woven deeply into the fabric of the Church's life, created the tinder that started the fire of the Holocaust. The Church argues that anti-Judaism, based on religion, is very different from Nazi anti-Semitism, which was rooted in the godless, twisted concept that the Jews are somehow an inferior, subhuman race. But that argument rings hollow, especially in light of the way too many Christians embraced the Final Solution enthusiastically and too many others stood by and let it happen.

Pope John XXIII, the most universally beloved pope of modern times, had begun to change all that. As a papal nuncio during the war, he had personally saved many hundreds of Jewish lives—acting under the instructions of Pius XII, according to Ronald Rychlak in his book, *Hitler, the War and the Pope* (Genesis Press, 2000). As the successor to Peter, he had eradicated the hateful reference to the "perfidious Jews" that had been part of the Good Friday liturgy for so many years. That language and the attitude it conveyed had made Good Friday a day to be dreaded for millions of Jews over hundreds of years. But Good Pope John had uprooted that language forever. On one Good Friday, when a Church official had accidentally lapsed into the old language in Pope John's presence, the pope had brought the liturgy to a momentary halt, in order to remind the official to use the new language. In this way and in many others, Pope John started the Church on the road to recognizing Jews as our elder brothers in the faith.

Now, John Paul was about to visit Yad Vashem, capping his own heroic efforts to heal centuries of Catholic-Jewish antagonism. As that visit approached and we discussed assignments for the day, we felt that one of us should travel to Tel Aviv and spend the afternoon with a group of survivors, as they watched the visit on television. My experience in interviewing survivors made me the logical choice.

So, early that day, I caught a cab and went to the home of Michal Schonbrun, the researcher in *Newsday's* Jerusalem bureau, who drove me and Miriam Sushman, a free-lance photographer, to Tel Aviv. Our destination was a local office of a privately funded organization called AMCHA, the National Israeli Center for Psychosocial Support of Survivors of the Holocaust and the Second Generation.

As we arrived, an AMCHA official named David Sealtiel greeted us at the door. We sat in a small office and talked about the needs of the 300,000 survivors in Israel and about the Christian family in Holland that saved Sealtiel's life by hiding him from the Nazis. Then Sealtiel left the office, and AMCHA officials ushered in another survivor, Esther Shon. She told us about escaping the Vilna ghetto in Lithuania. Her father had sewed a special pocket in his pants, so that he could smuggle her as he walked to his job outside the ghetto, then turn her over to a Catholic woman willing to hide her.

Next, we talked with Eva Gruber, whose mother carried her in a pail to hide her in a burned-out ritual bath. She told us about the gnawing hunger in the Lodz ghetto and about digging mass graves. We also spoke with Dr. Nathan Durst, the clinical director for AMCHA, whose work in helping survivors to cope with their pain has made him an expert on the way they deal with the Shoah, both physically and psychologically. One typical survivor reaction is anger.

"People cannot so easily cry. So they shout," Durst said. "People who are shouting are people in pain." Despite all the expectations by Jewish leaders about what the pope might say at Yad Vashem, Durst felt the pope's speech could not do much to relieve that pain. "My first reaction is that nothing would be helpful. We are talking about an immense evil."

As we waited together for the televised images of John Paul from Yad Vashem, the survivors were waiting to see a man who was still very much a stranger to them. Though polls showed that most Israelis viewed his visit favorably, it was also clear that most of them knew little about him. In contrast, I had come to know more about him than I ever thought I would.

When I started covering religion in 1993, I began studying him closely, as part of my work. Only two months later, I covered his visit to Denver. The following year, I sat in a Vatican audience hall and watched him meet with a small group of survivors. Following the formal speeches, he took the time to meet each of them personally. Most of them were Polish, and he spoke with them gently in the language they shared. As a Catholic, I remember feeling a great deal of pride in him in that audience hall, even as I tried to maintain my objectivity as a reporter. A few hours later, I sat a few feet away from John Paul and the chief rabbi of Rome during the historic Vatican concert for *Yom HaShoah*, Holocaust remembrance day.

At the close of the emotional concert, John Paul spoke about the Holocaust with great feeling. "I wish to invite all of you to observe a moment of silence in order to praise the Lord with the words which He will suggest to our hearts," he said, "and to hear once more the plea, 'Do not forget us!' "

Looking back at his brief talk on that occasion, it is striking how, in that great hall where the final notes of the concert had stopped sounding only a few minutes earlier, the pope used the theme of silence—a theme he would employ again to great effect on his visit to Yad Vashem. Thinking about silence in connection with the Holocaust, this conclusion seems inevitable: Before the fact, the silence of timidity and complicity helps ensure the triumph of evil. After the fact, a contemplative silence filled with contrition is a profoundly right response.

In 1995, John Paul visited New York, and I wrote a long piece about his life and travels that forced me to study him even more closely. In 1998, on the 20th anniversary of his election, I wrote an extensive assessment of his papacy. As his trip to Jerusalem neared, I wrote thousands more words of prepared obituary material. So, at the same time as my stories about survivors were broadening my knowledge of the Holocaust, my writing about John Paul was giving me a greater understanding of his wartime experiences and his attitudes toward the Jewish people.

Everyone knows that Karol Wojtyla is an immensely accomplished man who has lived a life of almost cinematic intensity and variety. His intellectual gifts have allowed him to produce an astonishingly vast body of writing: poetry, plays, philosophy, encyclicals, even a best-selling book, *Crossing the Threshold of Hope*. His almost preternatural energy has enabled him to reshape the papacy itself, from a pallid, stay-in-Rome-and-run-the-bureaucracy model to one that travels the world, speaking the Gospel in person to millions. His fidelity to his constantly restated theme, "Be not afraid," has emboldened him to stand up against totalitarianism and plant the seeds that led to the nonviolent fall of communism.

Before he achieved all this, the young Karol Wojtyla had gone through a personal, hands-on experience of the evils of Nazism. To avoid being sent off to a concentration camp, he had to work in a quarry. Still, he risked deportation to a camp by studying for the priesthood in a secret seminary and by participating in an underground theater company. He almost died when a Nazi truck ran him down. And worst of all, he had to watch as the Nazis rounded up many of his Jewish friends. Yet he did not perish. Viewed through the lens of John Paul's profound faith, this experience acquired an almost mystical meaning.

"I was spared much of the immense and horrible drama of the Second World War," he wrote in *Gift and Mystery*, his 1996 book on the 50th anniversary of his priestly ordination. "I could have been arrested any day, at home, in the stone quarry, in the plant, and taken away to a concentration camp. Sometimes I would ask myself: so many young people of my own age are losing their lives, *why not me?* Today I know that it was not mere chance. Amid the overwhelming evil of the war, everything in my own personal life was tending toward the good of my vocation. I cannot forget the kindnesses shown to me in that difficult period by people whom the Lord placed in my path, both the members of my family and my colleagues and friends."[6]

The pope developed an unshakable belief that *"my priesthood, even at its beginning, was in some way marked by the great sacrifice of countless men and women of my generation.* Providence spared me the most difficult experiences; and so my sense of indebtedness is all the greater, both to people whom I knew and to many more whom I did not know. . . ."[7]

All of this gave him a deeply human understanding of the Holocaust that no pope before him—and no pope who follows him—could possibly match. A real change in the church's often shameful attitude toward the Jews began when Pope John XXIII convoked the Second Vatican Council, which produced the landmark document *Nostra Aetate.* But it was John Paul who became the first pope to visit the synagogue in Rome, who established diplomatic relations between the Vatican and the State of Israel. Forcefully and repeatedly, John Paul had called anti-Semitism a sin. Like John XXIII, he referred to the Jews as our "elder brothers in the faith." And perhaps his closest friend, who dines with him regularly at the Vatican and still calls him by his childhood nickname of Lolek, is Jerzy Kluger, who grew up as a member of the once-thriving Jewish community in Wadowice, the pope's hometown.

In 1989, Kluger was involved in the unveiling of a plaque on the site of the synagogue where the Jews of Wadowice had prayed before the Nazis destroyed it. For that occasion, John Paul wrote him a letter in Polish, greeting his old friend with Kluger's childhood nickname, "Drogi Jurku" (Dear Jurek).

"If you are able to be there, in Wadowice, on the 9th of May, tell all who are gathered there, that, together with them, I venerate the memory of their so cruelly killed co-religionists and compatriots and also this place of worship, which the invaders destroyed," the pope wrote. "I embrace with deep reverence all those whom you are remembering this day. . . ." This letter, along with the deep friendship behind it, became the subject of *Letter to a Jewish Friend*, a 1994 book by Gian Franco Svidercoschi.[8]

As I took my seat with the survivors to watch the pope speak at Yad Vashem, I knew about his profound empathy with the Jewish people, I understood what he had already accomplished in healing the centuries-old enmity between Catholics and Jews, and I had witnessed some of the expectations that he carried with him to this day. Those expectations had begun to reach a crescendo just before he departed for the Holy Land.

On March 12, in a liturgy in Rome, the pope and Vatican leaders had publicly apologized for the failings of Catholics over the centuries. A few days later, on the Thursday before the pope's arrival, Rabbi Israel Meir Lau, the Ashkenazi chief rabbi of Israel, had met with reporters to discuss the visit. He pointed out that the pope had not mentioned the Holocaust in the March 12 liturgy. "He understood the Holocaust is not an event like other events to ask for forgiveness," Lau said. "It deserves a special treatment." In the Yad Vashem speech, Lau clearly expected, the pope would deliver that special treatment.

During that meeting with reporters, Lau spent a significant amount of time criticizing Pius XII. Though Jewish leaders had often praised Pius XII publicly for saving Jewish lives during World War II, a 1963 play called *The Deputy* had accused him of a guilty silence. Since then, many Jewish leaders have taken to criticizing the late pope in public and calling on John Paul to derail the canonization proceedings for him. Lau did not specifically say that he expected John Paul to rebuke his predecessor in the Yad Vashem speech. But Lau's criticism of Pius XII just before John Paul's arrival may have contributed to a mistaken public expectation that the Yad Vashem speech would somehow address such issues in detail.

Some Israelis, in fact, clearly felt that John Paul was just another in a long line of popes who had not exactly considered the welfare of the Jews a paramount concern. One group even carried a protest sign saying: "Where were you during the Holocaust?" The actual answer, of course, was that he was right in the middle of it. That sign was a symptom of a surprising lack of knowledge about this pope by many Israelis. In private conversations, I must admit, I have often criticized John Paul, reflecting the attitude of many women friends, both lay and vowed. Despite the eloquence of his language on the dignity of women in his 1995 *Letter to Women* and the 1988 apostolic letter *Mulieris Dignitatem,* they feel that the Church has not matched his words with action, has not paid women equally for their labor nor given them an equal opportunity for positions of influence that do not require ordination, and has resisted the use of inclusive-language scriptural translations. But I remember bristling when I learned of the "Where were you" sign. Whatever history's ultimate judgment on Pius XII, a judgment that must be delayed until all the documents have become available, it is difficult to see how any reasonable person can fail to see that John Paul has done more for Jewish-Catholic relations than any other pope in history—even more than Pope John XXIII.

Bearing the weight of unreasonable expectations and a limited understanding of his role in Catholic-Jewish relations, John Paul arrived at the vast and somber Hall of Remembrance. He began by restating the theme of silence that he had used at the Holocaust concert six years earlier.

"In this place of memories, the mind and heart and soul feel an extreme need for silence," the pope said. "Silence in which to remember. Silence in which to try to make some sense of the memories which come flooding back. Silence because there are no words strong enough to deplore the terrible tragedy of the *Shoah.*"

But the pope did not stop with silence. He went on to describe in simple language what had happened.

"I have come to Yad Vashem to pay homage to the millions of Jewish people who, stripped of everything, especially of their human dignity, were murdered in the Holocaust," John Paul said. "More than half a century has passed, but the memories remain.

"Here, as at Auschwitz and many other places in Europe, we are overcome by the echo of the heart-rending laments of so many. Men, women and children cry out to us from the depths of the horror that they knew. How can we fail to heed their cry? No one can forget or ignore what happened. No one can diminish its scale."

Those last words will stand for centuries to come as the Catholic Church's clear and ringing acknowledgement of the the horror of The Final Solution, no matter what the Holocaust deniers may try to say. Despite all the maneuvering in advance over expectations for the event, the frail pope's mere presence at Yad Vashem, his invocation of the Hebrew word *Shoah*, which many Jews prefer to the word Holocaust, and his brief but eloquent talk, with no new language and few specifics, moved people profoundly.

With the unblinking eye of the world focused on him, with his every word subject to later analysis and criticism, the pope did not deliver the precise, specific condemnation of the church's complicity that some Jewish leaders, such as Rabbi Lau, had hoped. In fact, as I listened and watched in Tel Aviv, surrounded by survivors, I found myself mentally rewriting his speech to add more specifics and make it more pointed and contrite. But the survivors themselves helped me to lay those ideas aside. Whatever the pope did not say, what he did do was to seize the dramatic moment, using as always his actor's feel for the stage and the audience, and amplifying it with his deeply felt emotions for the Jewish people. He shared in their silence before the awful mystery of this great evil, and he clearly shared in their pain. The survivors at AMCHA felt that sharing deeply.

Sitting before a television in Tel Aviv, that small group of survivors had not focused on the pope's exact choice of words, but they had seen right into the core of the event: He was there. A pope was standing in the Hall of Remembrance, with the names of the concentration camps arrayed all around him on the floor, and he was speaking with obvious emotion about the murder of European Jewry. In all the decades yet to come, the Holocaust deniers will not be able to wish away the palpable truth of a pope saying what John Paul said, with the shoes of the fisherman standing in a stark, sacred space where the names of the camps proclaim simply what human evil wrought there.

Along with then-Prime Minister Ehud Barak and others, the pope pauses at the memorial flame in the Hall of Remembrance at Yad Vashem.

© AP/WIDE WORLD PHOTOS

"What I hear is what never, ever a pope said before," said David Sealtiel, in the moments after the pope's speech. For Eva Gruber, his presence at Yad Vashem was decisive. "If he's coming here," she said, "he's doing the right thing."

Whatever John Paul's faults, his day in Yad Vashem is likely to remain forever a crucial element of any realistic assessment of his pontificate. No other pope had the background, the clarity of vision and the courage to do what he did for Catholic Jewish relations. And he did it. On this one trip, and especially on this one day, he rose above all the swirling politics around him and told the truth about the Holocaust. For all of Israel and all the world to see, the aging pope had shown himself to be what the record already demonstrated: the greatest pope the Jewish people ever had.

Jerusalem: Notre Dame Center

The Prayer

If the various religious communities in the Holy City and in the Holy Land succeed in living and working together in friendship and harmony, this will be of enormous benefit not only to themselves but to the whole cause of peace in this region. Jerusalem will truly be a City of Peace for all peoples. Then we will all repeat the words of the Prophet: 'Come, let us go up to the mountain of the Lord . . . that he may teach us his ways and that we may walk in his paths.' (Isaiah 2:3) To re-commit ourselves to such a task, and to do so in the Holy City of Jerusalem, is to ask God to look kindly on our efforts and bring them to a happy outcome. May the Almighty abundantly bless our common endeavors!

The Place

Notre Dame Pontifical Institute, opened in 1904 as a hostel for French pilgrims, is an imposing stone building a short walk from the New Gate to the walled Old City of Jerusalem. With a monastic touch in its décor but with an added measure of comfort, Notre Dame remains a popular hotel for pilgrims from around the world—an excellent and reasonable place to stay, to eat, or to attend Mass. During the papal visit, it was closed to the public to make room for John Paul's entourage from the Vatican. (The pope stayed with the nuncio, Archbishop Pietro Sambi, on the Mount of Olives.) The building suffered heavy damage in the 1967 war but was later repaired.

Reflection

By the time Pope John Paul II arrived at an auditorium in Notre Dame Center, he had every right to be weary. He'd started the day by celebrating a morning Mass beneath the vaulted ceilings of the Upper Room that is the traditional site of the Last Supper. As if that wasn't emotion enough for one day—to invoke the words of Christ, "This is my body," in such a place—he then went to Yad Vashem. And finally, his schedule called for him to appear at an interreligious ceremony called "Pray for the Peace of Jerusalem." Ceremonial gatherings with leaders of other faiths may be a routine and scripted event in the pope's life, but this one would prove to be more of an experience than expected.

Despite warnings from local church officials, Vatican planners of the papal trip very much wanted an interreligious meeting to be included on the pope's schedule—the picture of Muslim, Jewish and Christian leaders sharing the same stage in the Holy Land had the potential to be a powerful symbol and sign of hope. They, indeed, were following through on the pope's wishes, which were expressed in his 1994 letter *Tertio*

Millennio Adveniente. In it, John Paul had said that dialogue with Jews and Muslims should be an important part of the Jubilee Year of 2000, and that "attention is being given to finding ways of arranging historic meetings in places of exceptional symbolic importance"[9] such as Jerusalem. But given the awful rivalries, it proved difficult to arrange. Until the end, it was uncertain that a Muslim leader would consent to share the stage with Rabbi Lau. Ekrima Sa'id Sabri, the grand mufti of Jerusalem, declined to attend despite a great deal of coaxing.

At a gathering in the living room of his residence several days before the event, the mufti told a group of journalists crowded into chairs and sofas or on the carpeted floor that he was convinced the wrong message would get out if he went. Were he and the rabbi to pray together for peace, he said, it would be misconstrued as a sign that the present political situation in Jerusalem was acceptable.

I've been to plenty of news conferences in which there was an undercurrent of tension between the reporters and speaker—mayors in the midst of a corruption scandal, lawyers for celebrities accused of crimes. This one was memorable to me because there was such politeness, a thin glaze over the deep differences beneath.

The grand mufti had started out his remarks to the reporters with a call for honesty in the news media. He set it in the context of Muslim teaching, so it was more like getting a sermon than a dressing-down, but the point was clear: He had welcomed us into his residence on that quiet side street in Ramallah even though he didn't trust us. We carried the burden of representing the West. Later, he returned to that theme as he explained why he would not go to Notre Dame Center to be with the pope. "The media, they will twist the meeting . . . and show the world that everything is all right in Jerusalem. . . . The fact is there is an occupation against the Palestinians."

After the mufti declined, the Palestinian Authority arranged with church officials for the deputy leader of the religious court on the West Bank, Sheikh Taysir Tamimi, to attend. So the ceremony started off well enough, the pope seated on the stage of an auditorium with the rabbi to his right and the sheikh to his left. The audience they faced included a colorful mix of Roman Catholic cardinals, Orthodox and Eastern rite church leaders in their varied hats, rabbis, imams, and choirs of Jewish, Muslim and Christian children. A full-color, glossy, 16-page program was handed out, the cover featuring a lovely drawing of Jerusalem, the Muslims' Dome at the Rock standing out in its center in blue and gold. Inside were children's colorful drawings depicting scriptural passages about peace. The event began hopefully as a rabbi told the audience that while the pope's visit earlier in the day to Yad Vashem delved into the horrors of the past, this program was about hope for the future.

The event seemed to be going well as Rabbi Lau, speaking after a group of Jewish children sang part of Psalm 118 ("Blessed be he that cometh in the name of the Lord"), delivered remarks about Jerusalem as the "city of peace" (as its name indicates). But trouble began to develop when he praised the pope for "your visit here, your coming here, the recognition of the Jewish independent State of Israel, the recognition of Jerusalem as its united eternal capital city."

The rabbi was quite wrong in claiming that John Paul had recognized Jerusalem as Israel's "united" capital. In fact, the pope and Vatican diplomats wanted the holy places in Jerusalem under some form of international jurisdiction. A man in the audience—a church official later said it was Afif Safieh, a Catholic who is the Palestinian Authority's representative to the Vatican and the United Kingdom—shouted out immediately, notifying Rabbi Lau of his error.

It went from bad to worse when the sheikh spoke. Tamimi had looked uncomfortable as he sat on stage before the television cameras. Clearly, there was a strong current of opinion in the Muslim community against appearing in such a forum.

To applause, Tamimi welcomed the pope in Arabic to the "eternal capital" of Palestine and then in heated oratorical style denounced the "occupier," Israel. From the Jewish settlements on the West Bank to "genocide" to Jewish settler Baruch Goldstein's murder of Muslims praying at the Tomb of the Patriarchs in Hebron in 1994, Tamimi ran through a long list of grievances. Many people present or watching on television had no idea what he was saying because they didn't understand Arabic, but the angry tone said it all. Lau, who didn't understand the Arabic, certainly got the intended message. The *Jerusalem Post* reported Lau as saying that he leaned over to the pope and told him, "See what we have to deal with, see the atmosphere, see the blackmail."[10] Tamimi remained for John Paul's remarks and then, after whispering something to the pope (that he had another commitment, an official said), left before the ceremony was ended.

I've wondered what it would be like to be in the pope's shoes at that moment. For years, he had hoped for just such a meeting and now, the whole carefully set program was in tatters even though his remarks were still to be delivered. Everyone has experienced the embarrassment of having the best-laid plans go awry in public, but here the stakes were so large—a now unscripted and highly symbolic encounter was being played out on a stage before the world.

When the time arrived for the trio to plant an olive tree as a sign of peace, the sheikh was already gone, perhaps hoping to avoid such symbolism. Rabbi Lau also stepped back from participating. That left three pitchers of water and earth—so John Paul stepped up and emptied all of them.

The controversy served to fortify John Paul's speech, which had been written and handed out in advance. It gave a more immediate meaning to his observation that "not everything has been or will be easy in this co-existence" of three religions in Jerusalem. His solution was to focus on what the three religions agree upon, rather than on what divides. "We all agree that religion must be genuinely centered on God," he said. After quoting passages in the Quran—at one time, who would have expected to hear a pope quoting the Quran?—and Bible that praise God, he added: "In our times, when many are tempted to run their affairs without reference to God, the call to acknowledge the Creator of the universe and the Lord of history is essential in ensuring the well-being of individuals and the proper development of society."

It's worth stopping on that point. In a secular age, faith in God gives believers so much in common that it should overcome whatever divides them. I would add, too, that this should be true within the Christian churches. In reality, however, even Catholics—particularly bishops, priests, sisters and lay people who hold church jobs—are often divided along ideological lines, even though their religious faith gives them so much in common.

A quick story: A number of years ago, our newspaper hired writer Bill Reel, a columnist with great appeal among conservative Catholics. The list of issues on which Bill and I disagree is long. But it turned out that Bill's first day at the office was also my first on the religion beat, and we wound up sitting next to each other. I knew that Bill would be uncomfortable coming to work in a place like *Newsday*, which, at least by reputation, is a liberal newspaper. I'm sure many people looked at him as some iceman from the Stone Age because of his views on abortion, homosexuality, AIDS education, and family values. But having read his columns, I also sensed we had some common ground.

Boxes carrying files from my previous beat in the federal courthouse had arrived beside our desks, transported by a company called Choice Courier. All were marked "FOR

CHOICE." So I introduced myself to Bill and, pointing at the "FOR CHOICE" marks on all the boxes, told him that wasn't necessarily my position on abortion.

He laughed and we gradually got to know each other. What I found was that despite all the issues on which we cordially disagreed, the effort each of us made to put God at the center of our lives meant we were in accord on about 98 percent of what matters. Our sense of a shared faith tradition bound us in a special way in the rather secular world of a New York City newsroom. (I would not want to give the impression that a newsroom is devoid of religious faith. I was happily surprised when, after I became the religion writer, so many of my fellow reporters and editors spoke to me about their faith.)

Despite all that divides them, adherents to Islam, Judaism and Christianity still face the common task of coping with the advance of secularism and the purely rational mindset. The quarreling so evident that evening at Notre Dame Center is most damaging to religion, which many people see as a dividing force in the world. One night some years ago, I got a taste of just how intense this feeling against organized religion can be. An editor at the newspaper where I work hosted a series of discussion groups in her apartment in Manhattan, and I was invited to join one on the topic of religion. It soon became clear that I was nearly the lone believer in a group of people who were smarter and more articulate. It became my role to respond to their accusations that religion was invalid because it has been a factor in so much violence in the Middle East, northern Ireland and elsewhere. Many of those present were ethnically Jewish and I didn't have the necessary knowledge to defend their faith tradition. I wish religious leaders could hear more conversations like these.

The pope took this issue up in his remarks at Notre Dame Center, and the squabble between the sheikh and rabbi made his speech all the more apt. "Religion is the enemy of exclusion and discrimination, of hatred and rivalry, of violence and conflict," he said. "Religion is not, and must not become, an excuse for violence, particularly when religious identity coincides with cultural and ethnic identity."

Was anyone listening?

To underscore it, the pope emphasized: "Religion and peace go together!"

His point seems obvious, but it's worth reflecting on how often religion is used for a call to battle—and not just in the Middle East, but in contemporary American society too. Those who shun organized religion as a tool for division must be shown through example that they are seeing only a small part of the total picture.

Pope John Paul closed his remarks by referring to the Muslim, Jewish and Christian children who were a dramatic presence at the ceremony. He called them "a sign of hope and an incentive for us," adding, "Each new generation is a divine gift to the world."

He might have added that the children had behaved far better than the adults that evening.

As one church official later told me, the problem with the ceremony was that it was organized on a Western model, with its pleasant scenes of children of different faiths singing for peace. (Muslims don't have such a tradition for choral singing and so it was difficult to put together a choir; it included two Christian seminarians, perhaps the evening's best sign of interreligious cooperation.) But in the Middle East, where politics and religion go hand-in-hand, such a gathering was bound to be viewed as primarily political.

Shortly after the event, I spoke to a church official who had been involved with the interreligious ceremony, which, for news purposes, was little more than a footnote to the events at Yad Vashem earlier that day. It must have been awful, I thought, to be responsible for planning a papal event that went awry. But I was surprised to find he was rather upbeat. The reality of everyday life in the Holy Land had pierced the pomp and formality of a papal visit. It was good, the official said, for the pope to see that.

Questions for Reflection

1. How do you see the role and character of priests as you have observed them?

2. In what ways do our lives mirror the self-emptying of Jesus, and in what ways do we fall short of that difficult standard?

3. "I have become like a broken vessel," Psalm 31 says. In what ways did Pope John Paul II reflect that description? How did it help him to understand the *Shoah*?

4. What would you say to those who avoid organized religion because they feel it has played a role in violent conflicts?

5. Do you think there are ways in which Christian thinking still reflects the anti-Judaism of the past?

6. Would it have been better not to include an interreligious ceremony? Or were there useful lessons to be learned from it?

Chapter 5

Mount of the Beatitudes: Mass

After a helicopter flight from Jerusalem, John Paul offered Mass for about 100,000 people at the Mount of the Beatitudes, above the Sea of Galilee. Later, not far from the Mass site, in a tranquil church commemorating the Beatitudes, he met with Israeli Prime Minister Ehud Barak. Then, at Tabgha, on the lake's northeastern shore, he visited two places of pilgrimage, the Church of the Multiplication of the Loaves and Fishes and the Chapel of the Primacy of Peter. At this chapel, tradition holds, the resurrected Jesus appeared to his friends, grilled them a fish breakfast, and asked Peter to care for his flock. Finally, in Capernaum, where Jesus went to live after the arrest of John the Baptist, the pope visited a modern church built on what is believed to be the site of Peter's home. Bob wrote this chapter.

The Prayer

Not far from this very place Jesus called his first disciples, as he calls you now. His call has always demanded a choice between the two voices competing for your hearts even now on this hill, the choice between good and evil, between life and death. Which voice will the young people of the twenty-first century choose to follow? To put your faith in Jesus means choosing to believe what he says, no matter how strange it may seem, and choosing to reject the claims of evil, no matter how sensible or attractive they may seem.

The Place

Long before I stepped on the plane bound for Jerusalem, I had viewed covering the papal pilgrimage to the Holy Land as necessary but agonizing, a trial to be endured. One of my Irish genes has gifted me with a naturally pessimistic bent, always prepared to worry about the pitfalls and difficulties of an event that others anticipate as breathtakingly exciting.

Most reporters would have been elated to travel to the Holy Land at someone else's expense, to cover a world-historical event—not only the best religion story of the year, but one of the best in a long time. That was Paul's attitude: steady and upbeat. My memory of logistical nightmares during the coverage of earlier papal trips, however, predisposed me to stomach-churning anxiety. As the time for the trip approached, I was focusing not on history, but on fear.

One of those past nightmares had been the 1994 Holocaust concert in Rome conducted by Gilbert Levine, later knighted by the pope. It was an immensely important symbol in the history of Catholic-Jewish relations, and I now count myself lucky to have covered it. Nonetheless, at the time, I went through profound angst when *Newsday* decided at the last minute to send me to Rome. That decision came on a Monday, and my flight was to leave on Wednesday. Except for military service in Korea, I had never traveled outside North America, and I did not have a passport. That meant I had to spend the entire day on Tuesday navigating the passport bureaucracy in Manhattan. So I had little time to do advance reporting or confirm the arrangements in Rome.

On that Wednesday afternoon, I left for the airport with no firm guarantee that I'd even be able to gain admission to the concert that I was flying such a great distance to cover. Not surprisingly, this created a crushing fear of failure. The sleepless flight to Rome didn't help either. Between the time I had gotten up at home on Wednesday morning and the time I went to bed in my Rome hotel Thursday night, after covering the concert and writing my story, I was awake for about 36 hours.

Thankfully, I'd had the good sense to coordinate my flight plans with those of Monsignor Thomas Hartman, the director of radio and television for the Diocese of Rockville Centre. His connections and savvy helped me through the day. So did Roger Tilles, an influential Long Island real estate developer and one of the key fund-raisers for the concert, who handed me a ticket to the event as I arrived at the Vatican. So did Rabbi A. James Rudin of the American Jewish Committee. Just seeing the face of this wise man, a trusted source, cheered and energized me. The moment I caught sight of him in the Vatican, I blurted: "My rabbi!"

In the end, it all worked out fine, but I have never forgotten the anxiety. Nor do I have trouble remembering stomach-challenging moments during my coverage of papal visits to New York, St. Louis and Denver (where the security nightmares were so intense at Mile High Stadium that I lost a notebook for the only time in my career). In that tradition, the papal pilgrimage to the Holy Land seemed likely to be an obstacle course of tight security, difficult logistics, and sleep deprivation. To get myself through all that, I relied on a little mental trick, focusing on the aspect of the trip that most intrigued me: the Sea of Galilee. One could be skeptical about the exact location of this or that holy place, I kept telling myself, but the Sea of Galilee, after all, was the Sea of Galilee. As a Christian, I was truly eager to visit this historic lake, where it all began.

So, in our planning meetings before the pilgrimage, I had volunteered to write a scene-setting story about the Sea of Galilee. It would run in Friday's paper, the morning the pope was to celebrate Mass on the lakeside Mount of the Beatitudes, known in Israel as Mount Korazim. Late Thursday evening, I would take an overnight bus ride to the lake with parishioners from a small town in the West Bank, cover the Mass there, then move on to Nazareth, where the pope was to offer Mass on Saturday morning.

In the days leading up to the Sea of Galilee event, I had managed to set aside a little bit of time, in both Jerusalem and
Jordan, to work on my story about the lake. On Monday morning in Amman, I had briefly interviewed Cardinal William H.
Keeler of Baltimore, who had taken a helicopter ride over the
lake in 1989. "So much holy happened in this little piece of
land," he said. Late Wednesday, the night before I was to spend
the day in Tel Aviv with Holocaust survivors, I finished writing
the Sea of Galilee story.

Writing it, I had allowed myself to go a bit beyond the normal language of a news story and to express something of what
I felt about the lake and what it means to Christians. In conversations from my Jerusalem hotel room on Thursday evening
with the foreign editor, Tim Phelps, I had agreed to his request
that I recast the lead a little bit, to make it newsier. But he was
kind enough to let most of the rest of the story stand as I had
written it. I felt that it turned out well, and I'd like to quote a few
paragraphs here, to help set the scene for the pope's Mass:

"On the shores of the Sea of Galilee, Jesus asked a handful of rough-hewn fishermen to become fishers of men and
women, and they dropped everything to follow him.

In its surrounding towns and on its gentle hills, Jesus
preached in the synagogues, cured the sick, multiplied a
few loaves of bread and some fresh fish to feed thousands,
and delivered the most enduring sermon ever uttered.

On its waters, placid one moment and raging the next,
with waves driven by sudden winds from the dry wadis,
Jesus calmed a storm, strode across the troubled waters to
his fearful friends and climbed into a boat to find solitude,
when the demands of the crowd became too raucous.

And after his death, Jesus appeared to his still-grieving
followers, guided them to a plentiful catch, fixed them a
grilled fish breakfast and commanded Simon, renamed
Peter, to feed his sheep and lead his flock.

Now, Peter's current successor comes to the shores of
that sweet-water lake to break bread at a Mass on the traditional Mount of Beatitudes with as many as 100,000—the
largest event of his whole Middle East pilgrimage.

Spreading out below that gathering dominated by
young people, the lake has many names. In the Old
Testament, it is the Sea of Kinnereth. In the New Testament,
it is the Sea of Galilee, the Sea of Tiberias and the Lake of
Gennesaret. By any name, this lake is utterly central to the
life of Jesus and his disciples and to the rise of Christianity.

It is not simply the region where Jesus chose his followers, confirmed their leader and spelled out in the
Beatitudes his sermon on the way of life that he urged on
them. It is also a place that shaped him and his disciples.
Jesus suffered from the skepticism of others: an attitude
that nothing good could emerge from Nazareth. Peter had
such a strong Galilean accent that, when he tried to deny
that he knew Jesus, the accent gave him away.

Like Peter's accent, the spirit of Galilee has a way of
clinging to people, of making the Gospels more vivid,
amplifying the text with the texture of the land, the smell of
the lake, the gritty dust of the roads. . . ."

That was how I felt about the lake, and that attitude should
have been enough to sustain me through the difficulties of getting there. But the pilgrimage to the Sea of Galilee turned out
to be more stressful than I had imagined. The root of the difficulty was our decision that I should travel to the lake with a
group of Christian pilgrims from a West Bank village, rather
than catching a bus at the press center in Jerusalem and riding
north with other reporters. In theory, it made sense journalisti-
cally, because it gave me access to some people that I could get
to know along the way, instead of forcing me to seek quotes at
random in a crowd of 100,000 strangers. In fact, it turned out to
be a new pope-related nightmare for my memory bank.

My destination was a Christian Arab town called Taybeh, somewhere between Ramallah and Jericho on the West Bank. The researcher in the Jerusalem bureau, Michal Schonbrun, had made advance arrangements for me to ride north with a group of about 160 pilgrims. Now, I just had to get to the town square where they would be departing.

The first hurdle was an unavoidable fact of life in divided Jerusalem: I was simply not going to get a Jewish cab driver to pick me up at the Jerusalem Hilton and take me all the way to Taybeh. No destination on the Palestinian-controlled West Bank, especially late at night, seemed safe to an Israeli Jew. So, at 10:45 on Thursday night, at the end of a long day of travel back and forth to Tel Aviv, I took a short cab ride from the Hilton to the American Colony Hotel, in Arab East Jerusalem. There, I could catch a second cab, this one driven by a Palestinian. The driver's name, Michal had told me, was Kojak, just like the bald, lollipop-addicted detective in the gritty television series.

As I waited in the lobby for Kojak, I watched the rain and speculated about its effect on the Mass in the morning. I also wondered what I was doing here, in a setting that somehow reminded me of the film *Casablanca*, of Humphrey Bogart, of foreign intrigue. Some reporters, like Matt McAllester, the young Jerusalem bureau chief for *Newsday*, take naturally to working as foreign correspondents. As for me, my brief experiences in Rome in 1994 and in Jordan earlier in the week had convinced me that I cope poorly with unfamiliar surroundings, the complexities of getting from place to place in a foreign country, and the electronic-telephonic maze that seems always to stand between me and filing my story. So my apprehensions were high and my morale low.

Finally, Kojak picked me up and we headed out into the rainy night. In the dark back seat of the cab, on my cell phone, I answered questions from Tim Phelps on my Galilee and Yad

Vashem stories. As Kojak drove, it became clear that, unlike his namesake, he didn't have a clue. He had some vague idea where Taybeh was, but he wasn't exactly sure. So he had to stop several times to ask directions from other cabbies. Finally, I used my cell phone to call the parish where we were heading. Then I handed the phone to Kojak, so that the parish priest could give him directions in Arabic.

We reached the town square at a little after midnight, and I was relieved to see that the buses had not yet left. Inside the church, I watched as the Rev. Jack Abed, one of the priests leading the pilgrimage, called off names. We piled into the buses, which left just before 1 o'clock Friday morning. Father Jack handed out roses, plastic papal flags, and yellow scarves, with inscriptions in Arabic, Spanish and French: "Follow me" and "Here the Word was made flesh and dwelled among us." We were to wear these scarves as a way of sticking together in the huge crowd. Other groups would have similar scarves, but in different colors. Early in the bus ride, I decided it was too dark and too late for any interviewing here. That would have to wait until we arrived at the Sea of Galilee.

The bus ride seemed interminable, as people laughed, smoked and listened to loud Arabic music. It's possible that I nodded off for a moment along the way, but not much more than that. We stopped briefly for a bathroom break at 2:45, and I used the cell phone to call my wife, Judy, and tell her I was finally nearing the Sea of Galilee. As much as I longed to see the lake, at that moment in the dark of the bus, listening to the distant voice of my wife, I allowed my anxieties to overwhelm my pilgrim spirit. I wished that I were home.

Somewhere along the way, I learned later, the driver briefly got lost. We finally pulled into the long line leading to the parking lot at about 4:45. As the sun began to rise, someone on the bus did a passable imitation of a rooster crowing. Just before we finally reached our place in the parking lot, Father Jack issued some last-minute instructions in Arabic, and those who hadn't already put on their scarves began doing that. The bus finally parked just after 6 o'clock, five hours after we'd left Taybeh and an hour and a quarter after we'd first pulled into the line of buses. All around us, other groups, from all over the world, were disembarking and getting on line for the long trek up the hill from the parking lot to the Mass site.

As we walked up the hill, I interviewed Father Jack about the Christian community in Taybeh. While we talked, I looked below us and saw a peaceful-looking little building on the hillside sloping down to the lake. Later, I found out that it is a Franciscan-run shrine to the Beatitudes. Something about its peacefulness made me want to linger, but we continued to climb higher.

Our destination was a vast open field spread out below a massive, ugly new concrete structure at the summit. This building is the "Domus Galilaeae," the House of Galilee, which serves as a center for study, formation and retreat for a powerful renewal movement within the church called the Neo-Catechumenal Way. Many thousands of young "neos" from all over the world were among the huge crowd gathering for the Mass.

By the time we reached our assigned position, it was nearly 7 o'clock. As we looked up at the massive black tent that covered the elevated altar, we were off toward the right, not too far away from the altar and close enough to the other essential structure, the line of outdoor toilets. Our position was reasonably good, but the field was covered with mud. That made sitting impossible, except for those few who had brought along some sort of portable chair. So I resigned myself to standing the entire time.

In our group, I began to find people who spoke some English. They offered me food, in the spirit of Arab hospitality, and they gave me a sense of themselves and of their feelings about this event. The person I enjoyed interviewing most was Lydia Batarseh, then 64, who had grown up in Taybeh. Lydia had been living in Sterling Heights, a Detroit suburb, for many years, but she was back in Taybeh temporarily, caring for her sister during an illness. (Her sister died not long after the papal visit.) Since Lydia was in town, she was eager to make this journey to the Sea of Galilee. She had a lovely, simple personality, and a positive approach to this event. "As long as we see the pope, it doesn't matter where we stand," she said. "I love to do these pilgrimages. That's where you find the spirit of Christianity, everybody together from all over the world."

The crowd was truly international, including pilgrims from the United States, from Europe, from the Pacific Islands, as well as from Israel and neighboring countries. In that huge but peaceful assembly, I saw at least one reminder of the region's volatile politics: Right near our position, a group of young people carried a large banner about the suffering of the Arab Christians who had once lived in a small village called Kfar Bire'm, but had lost their homes during the 1948 struggle over the creation of the State of Israel. For the most part, though, this was a far less political, far more spiritual day for John Paul than the previous days had been.

As it turned out, it was more than three and a half hours from the time we arrived at our little square of mud until the popemobile came into view above us on the hill, at the other end of the huge field, near the Domus Galilaeae. Moments later, someone made an announcement, asking people to prepare for the Mass and to refrain from eating, drinking, smoking, or using cell phones. A few minutes past 11, the pope began the liturgy, and a light rain started falling soon after that.

Despite the warning announcement, people did eat and drink and even smoke during the Mass, which I found distracting. It is difficult to herd 100,000 people into a setting much like an open-air rock concert, make them wait four hours, then expect them to strike instantly a pose of total reverence, as if they were in a church. So I wondered how anyone could profit spiritually from this liturgy, with all these distractions and an intermittent rain falling from the sky. Still, whenever I'd look up and catch sight of Lydia Batarseh, standing as close as she could to the fence that separated our position from the altar area, I couldn't help but be impressed by her constant attitude of reverence and attention, no matter what was going on around her. Many more in that vast crowd, I'm sure, mirrored her prayerful attitude. And the pope more than did his part.

The pope blesses a vast throng gathered near the Mount of the Beatitudes for Mass.

Reflection

Just before noon, when John Paul started to deliver his homily, in English, his voice was as strong and resonant as I had heard it, on this or any previous trip. Something in his personality draws energy from the presence of young people, and they seem to respond to him too, despite the vast age and language gaps. He began it with what seemed a perfect Scripture verse for this very young crowd: "Consider your calling, brothers and sisters."[1] As his words echoed over the huge assembly on the hillside, it became clear that he was using this occasion, and this setting, to call the young people to something grand.

"Today these words of St. Paul are addressed to all of us who have come here to the Mount of the Beatitudes," the pope said. "We sit on this hill like the first disciples, and we listen to Jesus. In the stillness, we hear his gentle and urgent voice, as gentle as this land itself and as urgent as a call to choose between life and death.

"How many generations before us have been deeply moved by the Sermon on the Mount! How many young people down the centuries have gathered around Jesus to learn the words of eternal life, as you are gathered here today! How many young hearts have been inspired by the power of his personality and the compelling truth of his message! It is wonderful that you are here!" That line about "the power of his personality" resonated with me. Just a few days earlier, at the Wadi al-Kharrar, I had gained a sharper sense of the power of his personality by experiencing with my own senses the desert environment where he had submitted himself to baptism by John the Baptist, before going off alone for forty days to contemplate his mission.

"The first to hear the Beatitudes of Jesus bore in their hearts the memory of another mountain—Mount Sinai," the pope continued. "Just a month ago, I had the grace of going there, where God spoke to Moses and gave the Law, 'written with the finger of God' (Exodus 31:18) on the tablets of stone. These two mountains—Sinai and the Mount of the Beatitudes—offer us the roadmap of our Christian life and a summary of our responsibilities to God and neighbor. The Law and the Beatitudes together mark the path of the following of Christ and the royal road to spiritual maturity and freedom.

"The Ten Commandments of Sinai may seem negative," the pope said, listing examples such as the prohibitions against killing, stealing and committing adultery, among others. "But in fact they are supremely positive. Moving beyond the evil they name, they point the way to *the law of love* which is the first and greatest of the commandments: 'You will love the Lord your God with all your heart, all your soul and all your mind. . . . You will love your neighbor as yourself' (Matthew 22:37, 39). Jesus himself says that he came not to abolish but to fulfill the Law (Matthew 5:17). His message is new but it does not destroy what went before; it leads what went before to its fullest potential. Jesus teaches that the way of love brings the Law to fulfillment (Galatians 5:14). And he taught this enormously important truth on this hill here in Galilee."

John Paul quickly summarized the Beatitudes, the blessing that Jesus pronounced on those who are poor in spirit, gentle and merciful, those who mourn, who care for what is right, who are pure in heart, who make peace, who suffer persecution. "But the words of Jesus may seem strange," the pope continued. "It is strange that Jesus exalts those whom the world generally regards as weak. He says to them, 'Blessed are you who seem to be losers, because you are the true winners: the kingdom of heaven is yours!' Spoken by him who is 'gentle and humble in heart' (Matthew 11:29), these words present a challenge which demands a deep and abiding *metanoia* of the spirit, a great change of heart.

"You young people will understand why this change of heart is necessary! Because you are aware of another voice within you and all around you, a contradictory voice. It is a voice which says, 'Blessed are the proud and violent, those who prosper at any cost, who are unscrupulous, pitiless, devious, who make war not peace, and persecute those who stand in their way.' And this voice seems to make sense in a world where the violent often triumph and the devious seem to succeed. 'Yes,' says the voice of evil, 'they are the ones who win. Happy are they!'

"Jesus offers a very different message. Not far from this very place Jesus called his first disciples, as he calls you now. His call has always demanded a choice between the two voices competing for your hearts even now on this hill, the choice between good and evil, between life and death. Which voice will the young people of the twenty-first century choose to follow? To put your faith in Jesus means choosing to believe what he says, no matter how strange it may seem, and choosing to reject the claims of evil, no matter how sensible or attractive they may seem.

"In the end, Jesus does not merely speak the Beatitudes. He lives the Beatitudes. He is the Beatitudes. Looking at him you will see what it means to be poor in spirit, gentle and merciful, to mourn, to care for what is right, to be pure in heart, to make peace, to be persecuted. This is why he has the right to say, 'Come, follow *me*!' He does not say simply, 'Do what I say.' He says, "Come, follow *me*!'

"You hear his voice on this hill, and you believe what he says. But like the first disciples at the Sea of Galilee, you must leave your boats and nets behind, and that is never easy—especially when you face an uncertain future and are tempted to lose faith in your Christian heritage. To be good Christians may seem beyond your strength in today's world. But Jesus does not stand by and leave you alone to face the challenge. He is always with you to transform your weakness into strength. Trust him when he says: 'My grace is enough for you, for my power is made perfect in weakness' (2 Corinthians 12:9)!

"The disciples spent time with the Lord. They came to know and love him deeply. They discovered the meaning of what the Apostle Peter once said to Jesus: 'Lord, to whom shall we go? You have the words of eternal life' (John 6:68). They discovered that the words of eternal life are the words of Sinai and the words of the Beatitudes. And this is the message which they spread everywhere.

"At the moment of his Ascension Jesus gave his disciples a mission and this reassurance: 'All power in heaven and on earth has been given to me. Go, therefore, and make disciples of all nations . . . and behold I am with you always, until the end of the age' (Matthew 28:18-20). For two thousand years Christ's followers have carried out this mission. Now, at the dawn of the Third Millennium, it is your turn. It is your turn to go out into the world to preach the message of the Ten Commandments and the Beatitudes. When God speaks, he speaks of things which have the greatest importance for each person, for the people of the twenty-first century no less than those of the first century. The Ten Commandments and the Beatitudes speak of truth and goodness, of grace and freedom: of all that is necessary to enter Christ's Kingdom. Now it is your turn to be courageous apostles of that Kingdom!

"Young people of the Holy Land, young people of the world: answer the Lord with a heart that is willing and open! Willing and open, like the heart of the greatest daughter of Galilee, Mary, the Mother of Jesus. How did she respond? She said: 'I am the servant of the Lord, let it be done to me according to your word' (Luke 1:38).

"O Lord Jesus Christ, in this place that you knew and loved so well, listen to these generous young hearts! Continue to teach these young people the truth of the Commandments and the Beatitudes! Make them joyful witnesses to your truth and convinced apostles of your Kingdom! Be with them always, especially when following you and the Gospel becomes difficult and demanding! You will be their strength; you will be their victory!

"O Lord Jesus, you have made these young people your friends: keep them for ever close to you! Amen."

The circumstances had forced me to listen to this papal homily in a way that I ordinarily do not. Routinely, the Vatican press office distributes a copy of the homily to journalists shortly before the pope actually delivers it. That gives reporters an advantage. Those in the crowd have to listen to the homily without any printed words before them. We journalists can follow it, line by line, checking the spoken word against the prepared text, inserting any minor changes that the pope makes spontaneously. On this occasion, though, I was just one in the crowd. Since I hadn't taken the press bus from Jerusalem, I wasn't standing where most of the reporters were gathered, wherever that was. So I didn't have a prepared text.

As a result, I had to listen the same way everyone around me was listening, to pick up the sense and the sound of words as they bounced around that hillside. Perhaps I had to listen a little more carefully, because I was also taking notes as John Paul spoke. But without a text in front of me, I was free to experience this homily as a whole. Though its tone was aimed at the young people who predominated in that assembly, and I am well past young, this homily appealed to me viscerally in a way that other papal homilies had not. Standing on the hillside, my first impression was that much of its power flowed from the setting, where Jesus himself had preached so memorably. Later, when I had the full text in front of me, and I could examine it more carefully, I found that initial analysis confirmed.

Throughout the homily, John Paul made repeated place references, such as: "We sit on this hill like the first disciples, and we listen to Jesus." Then: "And he taught this enormously important truth on this hill here in Galilee." And: "You hear his voice on this hill, and you believe what he says." Clearly, his palpable sense of the presence of Jesus on this slope, leading down to the lake that Jesus loved, had brought life and vigor to his words. Just as clearly, he wanted the young people to draw energy from their presence at this specific latitude and longitude, where a young rabbi gave voice to ideas that have reverberated over two millennia. "Not far from this very place Jesus called his first disciples, as he calls you now," John Paul told the young people. "His call has always demanded a choice between the two voices competing for your hearts even now on this hill, the choice between good and evil, between life and death."

The essence of good homiletics is the ability to read life through the lens of Scripture. In this place, that lens seemed particularly clear. The pope did a masterful job of taking the familiar texts traditionally associated with this piece of geography and using them to examine the contemporary choices facing this assembly of young people at this moment in history. In the process, he nimbly blended words from their daily experience, such as "losers" and "winners," with loftier language, such as "metanoia," the "great change of heart" that Jesus calls us to make in the struggle of our lives. He skillfully wove the meaning of the two heights, Sinai and the Mount of the Beatitudes, into a reflection on Jesus and the law. And he cited a verse from the Gospel of John that I particularly love, because it records one of the high points in the up-and-down odyssey of Peter, my favorite among the apostles. Even as a teenager, I was so taken by his blend of maddening denseness, impetuosity and occasional searing insight that I took the name Peter at my confirmation. In this verse, Peter shines: "Lord, to whom can we go? You have the words of eternal life."[2]

The profound resonances of this place offered the pope a chance to build a connection between his hearers and the Jesus who walked this hillside, and he didn't miss. Despite the hubbub in that muddy field, I hope the young people took away from the homily some of the richness that he put into it. I suspect that most of them did not let the circumstances distract them as much as I allowed the confusion of the next several hours to muddy the clarity of my pilgrimage experience and to throw me "off message," as the politicians like to say.

Following a papal greeting to the young people—in Italian, French, German, Spanish, English, Polish, Hebrew, and Arabic—the Mass ended at 1:25, and I felt relieved. I had gotten through the trip north, elicited some insightful quotes from the people of Taybeh, and drawn some strong themes from John Paul's homily. So I knew I had a good story to write. All I had to do was find the press buses, and I'd probably be in Nazareth before 3 p.m. I could kick back, perhaps grab a short nap to catch up on the sleep I'd missed, and still have many hours to craft my story carefully. The deadline was 6 o'clock in the evening, and right now, it was still very early in the morning in New York.

The problem was this: I had no idea where the press buses were. Several times during the week, I had made inquiries about them. Would there be buses going directly from the Mount of the Beatitudes to Nazareth? Yes. Would I need a special ticket to get on them? No. They were somewhere, and I just had to locate them. This was where the Taybeh plan made the day more complex: If I had traveled north with the press buses, I'd have known exactly where they were. Of course, in that case, I wouldn't have met Lydia Batarseh or any of the other friendly folks from Taybeh.

Soon after the Mass ended, I found a woman from the government press office and asked her. She seemed a little harried and distracted, but she directed me to follow the other pilgrims back down to the large parking lot below, where we had begun our trek up the hill at 6 o'clock in the morning. At least, that's what I recall her saying to me. I followed her instructions, but when I finally reached the parking lot, I saw no signs for press buses. So I asked an Israeli policeman. His contribution was to make an expansive gesture toward the endless rows of buses and suggest grandly, but none too helpfully: "Here are all the buses."

That little moment of intense frustration was the first of many that afternoon. The one high point of these difficult hours was a brief glimpse of the papal motorcade rolling past, taking John Paul to the tranquil little church commemorating the Beatitudes, where he was to meet with Israeli Prime Minister Ehud Barak. Aside from watching him for a few moments, I spent the whole afternoon searching for transportation to Nazareth.

First, I trudged up and down the rows of buses, lugging the overnight bag that seemed to be growing heavier by the minute, and looking for any press bus signs. Nothing. Then I stood at the parking lot's exit, looking for signs on each departing bus. That was useless. I did draw encouragement from an encounter with a small group of journalists who were also looking in vain for the buses. As we talked, a police car drove by, and we flagged him down. The policemen offered to drive us back up the hill, to an area where the press buses might be. Unfortunately, once these journalists had climbed in, there was no room for me. So I asked one of them to call my cell phone when they had reached the top. Later, one of them did call me and told me the situation at the top of the hill was no clearer.

Through all this, I was growing increasingly more fatigued and frantic. By now, it was late Friday afternoon, and the Sabbath was drawing on. I had a good story to write, but no place to write and file it. Finally, after I had made a series of pleading phone calls to Matt and Paul, the government press office arranged for a police car to pick me up and drive me back up the hill. Just as I arrived there, a bus was leaving. It wasn't going to Nazareth, but to a kibbutz called Ein Gev. I had no

idea where Ein Gev was, but I was unwilling to risk watching
the bus drive off, then endure several more hours of waiting. So
I hopped on, not really sure whether I could get from Ein Gev
to Nazareth, or how long that might take. I was just grateful to
be on a vehicle of some sort and sitting down again, after so
many consecutive hours of standing.

As I discovered, Ein Gev is on the eastern shore of the Sea of
Galilee. Nazareth is on the opposite side, well beyond the
lake's western shore. Once I got off the bus at the kibbutz, I
began inquiring about transportation to Nazareth. Minutes
later, I encountered Steve Kloehn, a colleague from the *Chicago
Tribune* and Cindy Wooden of Catholic News Service. They told
me that some Associated Press photographers were in the cafeteria, editing their photographs, and they'd be leaving for
Nazareth before long. Sitting at a cafeteria table, with their lap-
tops plugged into an outlet above them, the photographers
weren't hard to find. I asked if they'd give me a lift to Nazareth,
and they said sure. At that moment, I finally felt relaxed, and I
realized I was starving. So, while I waited for them, I ordered a
dinner of St. Peter's fish and sat at a table near the photographers, unwilling to let them out of my sight.

As I ate my fish dinner, I looked out to the left at the waters
of the lake, calm in the dying light of early evening. After hours
of allowing myself to think about nothing but my logistical
predicament, I had time to remember how much I had longed
to see this lake. For too many hours, I had let the prose of logistics drown out the poetry of the Sea of Galilee. Now here it was,
a few feet away. A tide of emotions washed over me: relief that
I was finally going to get to Nazareth, regret that I had wasted
so much psychic energy on worry, and profound gratitude that
I was actually sitting at the side of this lake, seeing it with the
eyes of fact and of faith simultaneously. In that moment of
exhaustion and emotion, I felt tears welling up. Pilgrimage is
supposed to be difficult, I should have recalled, and at the end

of a day filled with anxiety, I was reaping a golden pilgrim moment.

During this late afternoon odyssey, I was completely out of touch with what the pope was doing, though I knew his schedule. Following the Mass for 100,000, the rest of his day involved no big crowds, no long homily, and very little politics. He visited briefly on the Mount of the Beatitudes with Barak, who expressed the hope that the pope's visit would help the peace process. From there, the pope turned his eyes entirely away from the political dimensions of the journey, focusing the rest of his day on prayerful, low-key visits to important spiritual pilgrimage sites along the shore of the lake.

At Tabgha, an Arabic contraction for the Greek word *Heptapegon*, "place of seven springs," the pope visited the Church of the Multiplication of Loaves and Fishes. The current church was consecrated in 1982,[3] but it follows the plans of a fifth-century church that had been built above an earlier fourth-century chapel. Its famous feature is a restored mosaic of two fish on either side of a basket of bread, recalling the five barley loaves and two fish that Jesus used to feed a large crowd in this area.

A short distance away, on the lake shore, John Paul visited a little chapel, built in 1933 on the site of earlier shrines, commemorating the primacy of Peter. Here, tradition holds, the resurrected Jesus appeared to his friends, grilled them a fish breakfast, and closely questioned the man who would lead his followers. "When they had finished breakfast, Jesus said to Simon Peter, 'Simon son of John, do you love me more than these?' He said to him, 'Yes, Lord; you know that I love you.' Jesus said to him. 'Feed my lambs.' A second time he said to him, 'Simon son of John, do you love me?' He said to him, 'Yes, Lord; you know that I love you.' Jesus said to him, 'Tend my sheep.' He said to him the third time, 'Simon son of John, do you love me?' Peter felt hurt because he said to him the third time, 'Do you love me?' And he said to him, 'Lord, you know everything; you know that I love you.' Jesus said to him, 'Feed my sheep . . .' "[4] Inside the church, John Paul kissed a rock where Jesus is believed to have served this momentous breakfast.

From Tabgha, the pope journeyed about a mile and a half north along the shore to Capernaum (from the Hebrew, *Kfar Nahum*, the village of Nahum). During the lifetime of Jesus, this tiny fishing village had a small Roman garrison and a customs post. At its tax booth, Jesus encountered a tax collector named Matthew (called Levi in Mark and Luke) and summoned him gently but undeniably: "Follow me."[5] The village was the home of Simon Peter, his brother Andrew, and the two sons of Zebedee, James and John. After the arrest of John the Baptist, Jesus himself left Nazareth and lived in Capernaum at the start of his ministry.[6]

Here, Jesus preached in the synagogue and "astounded" the simple people of the area with his wisdom.[7] Here, he cured a paralytic lowered through an opening in the roof,[8] cast out a demon,[9] and cured the son of a royal official.[10] Here, Jesus rebuked his disciples for arguing over who would be the greatest in his kingdom, telling them: "Whoever wants to be first must be last of all and servant of all."[11] Here, in the synagogue, he uttered these astonishing words: "Very truly, I tell you, unless you eat the flesh of the Son of Man and drink his blood, you have no life in you."[12] Here, a centurion met Jesus and asked him to cure his ailing servant. The centurion said something that still echoes in the eucharistic liturgy: "Lord, I am not worthy to have you come under my roof; but only speak the word, and my servant will be healed."[13] Moved by this soldier's powerful faith, Jesus healed his servant.

Despite all the miracles that he worked in Capernaum, Jesus expressed exasperation over the unbelief of the people, in sharp contrast to the faith of the centurion. "If the deeds of power done in you had been done in Sodom, it would have remained until this day. But I tell you that on the day of judgment it will be more tolerable for the land of Sodom than for you."[14] The village, seriously damaged in an earthquake in 746, had to be rebuilt a short distance to the northeast of its original site. By the eleventh century, it had been abandoned.

At twilight on this Friday afternoon, John Paul visited a modern church at the site of a fifth-century structure, constructed around a one-room dwelling from the first century. Tradition holds that this is the site of Peter's home. As the pope sat there in prayer, those accompanying him sang *"Tu es Petrus,"* Latin for "You are Peter."

While all this was going on, Paul was monitoring the pope's progress from the press center in Jerusalem, and I was on the other side of the lake, still waiting for my connection to Nazareth. Though the pope didn't say anything significant at the chapel of the primacy in Tabgha or at the church of Peter's house in Capernaum, it is not difficult to imagine those sites as the setting for some future ecumenical gathering to discuss the role of the papacy, the Petrine ministry, in Christianity.

It was John Paul himself who raised this knotty subject in his 1995 encyclical on Christian unity, *Ut Unum Sint* (That They May Be One), the first papal encyclical ever to address ecumenism as its primary concern. In the document, the pope acknowledged that the papacy had become associated in the minds of many Christians with "painful recollections,"[15] and he added: "To the extent that we are responsible for these, I join my Predecessor Paul VI in asking forgiveness." Later, he expressed a willingness, even a sense of obligation, "to find a way of exercising the primacy which, while in no way renouncing what is essential to its mission, is nonetheless open to a new situation."[16] And he added: "This is an immense task, which we cannot refuse and which I cannot carry out by myself. Could not the real but imperfect communion existing between us persuade Church leaders and their theologians to engage with me in a patient and fraternal dialogue in which, leaving useless controversies behind, we could listen to one another, keeping before us only the will of Christ for his Church and allowing ourselves to be deeply moved by his plea 'that they may all be one . . . so that the world may believe that you have sent me' (John 17:21)?"[17]

The following year, the retired archbishop of San Francisco, John R. Quinn, gave a lecture on papal primacy at Oxford University. The occasion was the dedication of Oxford's Campion Hall, named for the Jesuit Edmund Campion, and Quinn reminded his audience that Campion "was put to death precisely because he would not repudiate the primacy"[18] of the bishop of Rome. "The pope has asked us for an honest and serious critique,"[19] Quinn said. "He has every right to expect that this call will be heard and that this response will be especially forthcoming from those who recognize and reverence the primacy of the Roman Pontiff—as the church searches out the will of God in the new millennium that is before us."

Quinn suggested reform in the Church's style of governance, as opposed to its substance. One area he cited was the Roman Curia, the Vatican's bureaucracy. Though Quinn conceded the necessity for the Curia and praised the quality of many of its staff, he offered a significant critique. "Yet it must be honestly acknowledged that many Orthodox and other Christians are hesitant about full communion with the Holy See not so much because they see some doctrinal issues as unsolvable, not because of unfortunate and reprehensible historical events, but precisely because of the way issues are dealt with by the Curia," Quinn said. "The concern has to do with the appointment of bishops, the approval of documents such as *The Catechism of the Catholic Church*, the grave decline in the numbers of priests and the consequent decline in the availability of Mass for the people,

the cognate issue of the celibacy of the clergy, the role of episco-
pal conferences, the role of women and the issue of the ordination of women. Two things are involved in these issues: the decision of the Holy See on a specific issue and the way in which
these decisions are reached and implemented. For instance, are
such decisions imposed without consultation with the episcopate and without appropriate dialogue? Are bishops appointed
against an overwhelming objection of people and priests in a
given diocese? Where the answer to these and other such questions is affirmative there are serious difficulties for Christian
unity."[20]

In published reports, the descriptions of Quinn's lecture
made it sound more like criticism than dialogue, and some
bishops felt the need to respond publicly. The most visible was
Cardinal John O'Connor of New York. Writing in the arch-
diocesan newspaper, *Catholic New York,* O'Connor made sure to
point out that he considered Quinn a friend, one who "has a
special, indeed, a reverent affection for the pope he is perceived
as criticizing in his lecture," and a respect "for the Roman Curia
he is seen as censuring, at times, rather severely." Still,
O'Connor differed with Quinn on several issues, including
Quinn's interpretation of what the pope had meant by his reference to primacy. "I had personally interpreted the pope's call
to dialogue in this encyclical as an invitation to 'church leaders
and their theologians' of other Christian persuasion, rather
than to Roman Catholics," O'Connor wrote. "Archbishop
Quinn clearly considers it to be a call to Roman Catholic bishops, theologians and others to make recommendations to the
pope. I'm not sure our differences in interpretation are unimportant."[21]

The Quinn lecture also drew responses from other bishops,
such as Archbishop Rembert Weakland of Milwaukee and
Bishop James T. McHugh, then the bishop of Camden, New
Jersey, and later of Rockville Centre, on Long Island. Beyond

that, in the five years between *Ut Unum Sint* and John Paul's visit to the Holy Land, the public dialogue on the primacy did not get much further. Whether it unfolds more fully in the near future may well depend on John Paul's successor, who will inherit a papacy very different from the one that existed in 1978, when Cardinal Karol Wojtyla of Kraków was elected and took the name John Paul II.

So John Paul's call for a cooperative rethinking of the form of the primacy remains an unfinished piece of business for the Church. Whether the next steps take place during his pontificate, or whether they await the election of his successor, would it not be a wonderful piece of symbolism if some element of that debate, if only a ceremonial opening or closing, took place at one of the sites that John Paul visited on that Friday afternoon in March, at Capernaum or at Tabgha?

Questions for Reflection

1. What have you learned from the occasions when you allowed the prose of logistics to distract you from the poetry of a potentially glorious moment, as I did at the Sea of Galilee?

2. Are there places in the Holy Land that you long to visit, to heighten your understanding of the Gospel? What are they? What is it about them that appeals to you?

3. Do you practice what St. Ignatius Loyola recommended: a meditative reading of Scripture, fully engaging your imagination to make the text come alive in your mind?

4. In his homily at the Mount of the Beatitudes, John Paul told the young people, in the words of St. Paul, "Consider your calling, brothers and sisters." How often do you consider your calling, reflecting carefully on where you are going in life and whether your goals are Gospel goals?

5. In *Ut Unum Sint,* John Paul raised the question of papal primacy. If you were able to speak with him in a private audience, what would you say to him about the best way for any pope to exercise his primacy?

Chapter 6

Saturday, March 25, 2000

Nazareth: Basilica of the Annunciation

An intense devotion to Mary has always been at the center of John Paul's spirituality. So this day, beginning with a visit to the Basilica of the Annunciation, which commemorates Mary's profound act of obedience to God's will, was a deeply meaningful one for him. Later, the pope prayed in a modern church at the site of the Garden of Gethsemane, where Jesus prayed in agony the night before he died. John Paul ended his public day with a difficult ecumenical gathering hosted by Diodoros I, the Greek Orthodox patriarch of Jerusalem. Bob wrote this chapter.

The Prayer

In Nazareth where Jesus began his public ministry, I ask Mary to help the Church everywhere to preach the "good news" to the poor, as he did (Luke 4:18). In this "year of the Lord's favor," I ask her to teach us the way of humble and joyful obedience to the Gospel in the service of our brothers and sisters, without preferences and without prejudices.

The Place

In the infancy and early childhood of Jesus, the Gospel of Matthew tells us, the terrors of power politics played a major role. Matthew describes an angel appearing to Joseph in a dream and warning him to take Mary and Jesus to Egypt, to escape King Herod, who was worried that the prophesied newborn king of the Jews would become a threat to his own throne. "This was to fulfill what had been spoken by the Lord through the prophet, 'Out of Egypt I have called my son.' "[1]

Herod had learned of the new king's birth from three visiting wise men. Enraged that they had failed to return and tell
him where to find the child, Herod ordered the murder of
every boy in Bethlehem under the age of two.[2] Later, after the
king's death, another angelic appearance prompted Joseph to
take his family to Galilee. "There he made his home in a town
called Nazareth, so that what had been spoken through the
prophets might be fulfilled, 'He will be called a Nazorean' "[3]

Every Christian knows this story, reported only in the
Gospel of Matthew, and those familiar with mainstream
Scripture scholarship know that many scholars question
whether it is historical. They have found no independent evidence of the slaughter at Bethlehem, for example, in the writings of the usually reliable Jewish historian, Flavius Josephus.
(But Josephus does say that Herod, one of the nastiest characters in Scripture, ordered his soldiers to murder political prisoners at the time of his own death, just to be sure that his passing would provoke mourning.)[4] Some scholars think that
Matthew included the flight story in his infancy narrative to
make a point, such as drawing a parallel between the escape of
Jesus from Herod and the escape of Moses from the pharaoh.[5]
So there are legitimate uncertainties about the origins of this
familiar passage. But this much seems utterly certain to me: If
Jesus, Mary and Joseph did indeed spend many months in
exile before arriving at this modest town in Galilee, they could
not have been happier to see it, at long last, than I was, at the
end of my day of frustration on the Sea of Galilee.

Not long after I had finished my supper of St. Peter's fish in
the cafeteria at the kibbutz Ein Gev, the two photographers
who had agreed to drive me to Nazareth appeared ready to
leave, but with a slight change of plans. One took his car and
left for Jerusalem. The other, an Italian, arranged a ride with a
veteran photographer, Moshe Milner of the government press
office. I joined them, reaching my room in Nazareth at 8:30,

seven hours after the Mass on the Mount of the Beatitudes had ended.

By now, it was about 37 hours since the last time I had been in bed, at the Jerusalem Hilton. Since then, I had traveled to Tel Aviv to meet with the Holocaust survivors, written the story, caught two cabs to Taybeh, ridden the bus all night to the Sea of Galilee, covered the papal Mass, endured hours of uncertainty at the parking lot, hopped on a bus to Ein Gev, and finally had my few moments of peace with the lake and all the images it evoked. So, by the time I reached my hotel room and sat down to write, I had to fight to keep my eyes open. At one point, I actually fell asleep while writing, and awoke to find myself typing Matt McAllester's name into my story. But I shook myself awake, finished the story, and dictated it to Paul in Jerusalem, so that he could add to it. Then I fell into a deep sleep, in my comfortable hotel room in the town where Jesus grew to manhood and ministry.

On Saturday morning, I walked out of my hotel and headed for the towering, distinctive dome of the Basilica of the Annunciation. Once again, I was not part of the tiny press pool. So I was not allowed inside the basilica for the papal Mass. Paul would be watching that from the press center in Jerusalem and writing the top of the story. My job was to get him some color and quotes in the streets surrounding the basilica. I would not have the opportunity to see the inside of this amazing church during the Mass, and I wouldn't have the time to visit it after the pope had left.

In an unusual way, the basilica celebrates the flesh-and-blood mystery of the Incarnation in a symphony of stone, blending together on different levels the ancient and the new, the early Christian churches and an imposing work of twentieth-century church architecture. Before the Mass, the pope experienced all of them: the twelfth-century Crusader-era church, the fifth-century Byzantine church below it, and the grotto below, which tradition records as the place where the angel Gabriel announced to Mary that she was to become the *Theotokos*, the Mother of God.[6] In the grotto, a simple Latin inscription describes in spare language the significance of this place in the breathtaking mystery of the Incarnation: *"Hic verbum caro factum est."* Here, the Word became flesh.

A prayerful moment during the papal Mass at the Basilica of the Annunciation in Nazareth.

Somehow, though archaeological evidence shows that Christians venerated this spot from the second and third centuries, it doesn't really seem to matter whether the angelic apparition happened precisely here or a few hundred yards away. This is the place where tradition celebrates Mary's unflinching "yes" to the angel's announcement. Here, John Paul knelt intently in prayer, then left behind a golden rose as a token of his intense devotion to Mary. Years earlier, at the Marian shrine in Fatima, he had deposited a much more personal memento: a bullet that had nearly ended his life during the 1981 assassination attempt in St. Peter's Square on May 13, the anniversary of Mary's first apparition before three little children in a small village in Portugal. This pope does not believe in coincidences, and from the time of the assassination attempt, he has always believed that Mary saved his life.[7] Long before that event and this pilgrimage, a powerful devotion to Mary had been at the heart of John Paul's spirituality. He saw her as the first disciple of Jesus and a model for all future disciples and for the Church itself. So his visit to the grotto of the Annunciation was one of the crowning moments of his pilgrimage.

This largest Catholic church in the Middle East is a stunningly grand edifice for a city with such humble origins. Nazareth began as an agricultural village, too insignificant to rate mention in lists of Galilean towns found in the Talmud or in the work of Josephus. It is now the most populous Arab city in Israel. Even before the outbreak of lethal conflicts throughout Israel in the fall of 2000, Nazareth had become a focal point of Muslim-Christian-Jewish impasse.

A few minutes after leaving my hotel, I encountered the small, hotly contested piece of real estate that lies at the heart of the crisis. On the street leading up to the basilica, someone had strung up a large sign: "Moslem Mosque on Moslem Land/Every Believer Should Give a Hand." By the time I arrived, the pope was already inside the basilica. After the

Mass, he would be riding down this street in his popemobile, passing this sign. It was not there as a challenge to John Paul, but simply to point out to him that this was the site, very close to the basilica, where the Muslim community wanted to build a small mosque, marking the grave of a nephew of Saladin, the Muslim warrior who beat back the Crusaders in the twelfth century.

In the modest square behind the sign, where Muslims were gathering for noon prayer, I talked with Ghneim Abed, a local insurance agent who also plays a local role in caring for the *waqf*, land that the Muslims consider set apart as holy. Some Christians had objected vehemently to the construction of a mosque so close to the basilica, but the government had intervened and worked out what some called a compromise. Though the Muslims accepted those terms, many Christians remained angry, feeling that the Israeli government had broken its promise. "This is sacred land," Abed said, explaining that it cannot be sold or used for anything but religious uses. "It was confiscated by the Israeli government in 1948. It is between us and the Israeli government." Under the agreement, the Muslims would build the mosque and set aside a small adjoining square as a gathering place. This space would be open to the public, but in the minds of the Muslims, it would remain part of the *waqf*.

A few days earlier, Paul had attended a gathering at the home of Grand Mufti Ekrima Sa'id Sabri, in Ramallah, on the West Bank. The mufti had talked about the mosque, insisting that the issue had been resolved locally in Nazareth, despite outside agitation by forces that included the media. Cardinal William H. Keeler of Baltimore, who traveled to the mufti's house with the journalists attending our religion and the media conference, gently took issue with that assessment. "The Christians from within still have some serious problems with it," he told the mufti.

Though many Nazareth Christians still objected to the mosque, and the Vatican had not abandoned hope of reversing the decision, Abed seemed to feel that the compromise had enabled everyone to get past the controversy. "I would say that we are in the process of going back to the regular relationship that has been existing in this area for hundreds of years," he said. "That's our wishes, that the visit will contribute to better understanding and to helping people go back to their normal relationships."

That Muslim wish was not the only burden of hope that greeted John Paul in Nazareth. The dwindling Christian community, for example, hoped that his visit would bolster morale. And a few feet away from the mosque site, I encountered two young businessmen relaxing at a small table in a sidewalk cafe and hoping that the pope's pilgrimage would eventually draw more Catholic pilgrims to this city, where their company manages two luxury hotels.

Turning my attention away from these earnest young entrepreneurs, I walked closer to the mosque site and the basilica, just before noon. A large number of Muslims in the square knelt in prayer, touching their foreheads to the ground in the traditional gesture of reverence. The chant of praise, *"Allahu akbar,"* meaning "God is great," filled the square. At the same time, the bells of the basilica rang out the notes of a familiar Marian hymn, and the words of the refrain, echoing the salutation of the angel, rang in my head: *"Ave, ave, ave, Maria."*

Not long after that, the popemobile rolled down the street, past the mosque site, past the enthusiastic crowd of Muslims and Christians, and past the two hopeful hotel managers. On the sidewalk, tightly pressed in by the crowd on all sides, I was less than thirty feet away from the pope, which was as close as I came to him during the entire week. The pope's passage took only a few moments, and as soon as he had gone, I did a few more interviews, including a young man wearing a blue scarf

just like the yellow one my little group at Taybeh had worn to
the Mass in Galilee the day before, with its inscription: "Here
the Word was made flesh and dwelled among us." His name
was Nasif Lawen, and he lived in Nazareth. The day before, he
had gone to the Mount of the Beatitudes for the papal Mass.
"The pope means a lot to us," Lawen told me, as the crowd
began to disperse. "I think that he's the first man in the world—
number one."

Then I was ready to leave the basilica area and arrange my
transportation from Nazareth to Jerusalem. But first, I called
Paul on the cell phone, and he said that the story could use an
interview with someone who had been at the Mass, inside the
basilica. The streets were still streaming with the people who
had stood on the sidewalks watching the pope's departure, and
I wasn't sure how I was going to tell them apart from those
who had been inside. But as I walked toward the basilica, along
the same street where I had watched the popemobile, I figured
it out.

Over the years, I've been to enough special liturgies to know
that liturgists almost always produce a take-home booklet con-
taining the Scripture readings and the words of the hymns. I
stopped a gentleman carrying one of these little booklets, and I
asked him about the Mass. He spoke with me briefly, told me
he had sung in the choir, then pointed out a distinguished-
looking man walking past us, away from the basilica. So I interviewed him too. His name was Joseph Khill, and he had directed the 100-voice choir at the Mass. It was a proud and historic
day for him. Not only had he led the choir and received
Communion directly from the hands of the pope, but his son,
Bishara, had played the organ. Bishara is Arabic for annunciation. So someone named Annunciation had played the organ in
the Basilica of the Annunciation, on March 25, the Solemnity of
the Annunciation, for a pope who made Mary's courageous
response to the angelic announcement a central theme of his

homily, just as Mary has been a pivotal focus of his own spirituality.

Reflection

At the start of his homily, the pope underlined the importance of this visit to Nazareth. "I have longed to come back to the town of Jesus, to feel once again, in contact with this place, the presence of the woman of whom Saint Augustine wrote: 'He chose the mother he had created; he created the mother he had chosen,' " the pope said.

John Paul reminded the congregation at the basilica, and the millions watching all around the world, that he had begun his journey in spirit with a recollection of Abraham, who also assented to a difficult call. "That journey has brought us today to Nazareth, where we meet Mary, the truest daughter of Abraham," the pope said. "It is Mary above all others who can teach us what it means to live the faith of 'our father.' In many ways, Mary is clearly different from Abraham; but in deeper ways 'the friend of God' (Isaiah 41:8) and the young woman of Nazareth are very alike.

"Both receive a wonderful promise from God. Abraham was to be the father of a son, from whom there would come a great nation. Mary is to be the Mother of a Son who would be the Messiah, the Anointed One. 'Listen!', Gabriel says, 'You are to conceive and bear a son. . . . The Lord God will give him the throne of his ancestor David . . . and his reign will have no end' (Luke 1:31-33).

"For both Abraham and Mary, the divine promise comes as something completely unexpected. God disrupts the daily course of their lives, overturning its settled rhythms and conventional expectations. For both Abraham and Mary, the promise seems impossible. Abraham's wife Sarah was barren, and Mary is not yet married: 'How can this come about,' she asks, 'since I am a virgin?' (Luke 1:34)" The pope neatly summed up the decision facing both the patriarch and the teenager: "Like Abraham, Mary is asked to say yes to something that has never happened before."

Still, Mary said yes, an assent that was more difficult than we can possibly appreciate today. Even in the Nazareth of the year 2000, a fair-sized city with many distractions beyond gossip, a story can find its way around. But in the tiny village of Mary's youth, with a minuscule population and few forms of entertainment more compelling than tales told at the side of the well, news of an unwed teenager's pregnancy would have flown around town at lightning speed. The consequences might have been more than mere gossip. The news could have triggered a stoning. As a pious Jew, Mary certainly knew that, and she knew that the miraculous origins of her embarrassing condition would not necessarily deflect the scorn of her small community. In effect, she was staking more than just her reputation on God's promise that it would all work out. She was betting her very life.

For me, the story of Mary's bravery at the Annunciation has always been a fruitful subject for meditation. At one time in my life, I felt a calling to priesthood. By the end of high school, I had determined that my true vocation was actually journalism. Still, the whole question of calling has always been a powerful one for me. As a young man, I grew to love the courageous Latin affirmation that candidates for priesthood intoned at ordination: *"Adsum."* That potent word means, simply, "Here I am," an unambiguous assent to God's call, echoing the language of Isaiah 6:8. That word has always moved me. Similarly, one of my favorite hymns is about calling. It offers a dialogue between God, who asks plaintively, "Whom shall I send?" and the faithful, who answer stoutly, "Here I am, Lord."[8]

Answering God's call can be a costly decision, the martyrs have taught us. As children, we looked at the example of long-ago martyrs. As adults, we learn that we don't have to look very far away or very long ago to find encouragement in people who answered the call and remained steadfast, despite the danger and the doubt. These days, I am thinking specifically of the four women murdered for their service to the poor in El Salvador: two Maryknoll nuns, Maura Clarke and Ita Ford, an Ursuline nun, Dorothy Kazel, and a lay missioner, Jean Donovan. They died on December 2, 1980, because a military-dominated government saw service to the poor not as faithful witness to the Gospel, but as a communist plot. [9] Right now, as I write these words, the twentieth anniversary of that horrible event is only a few days away, and I have been writing a story for *Newsday* about their lasting significance.

Maura Clarke and Ita Ford grew up not far from where I did—Maura in Belle Harbor, along the ocean in southern Queens, and Ita in Brooklyn. So I naturally focus on them even more than on Dorothy or Jean. They appeared very different, Maura towering over the elfin Ita, but they shared a great strength and a clear vision of the dangers that faced them.

"My fear of death is being challenged constantly as children, lovely young girls, old people are being shot and some cut up with machetes and bodies thrown by the road and people prohibited from burying them," Maura wrote during her brief three months in El Salvador, after serving for nearly two decades in Nicaragua. "One cries out: Lord how long? And then too what creeps into my mind is the little fear, or big, that when it touches me very personally, will I be faithful?"[10]

Maura had come to El Salvador because she felt drawn by the preaching of Archbishop Oscar Arnulfo Romero, who met his own martyrdom on March 24, 1980. (John Paul's relationship with Romero will not be recalled as a highlight of his pontificate. The pope felt that Romero was too much in the thrall of liberation theology, which John Paul saw as too willing to accept Marxist analysis and Marxist revolutionary solutions. Three years after the assassination, John Paul visited Romero's grave.[11] While the archbishop was still alive, however, the pope had moved him to tears by pointedly keeping him waiting for days for a meeting at the Vatican, then counseling Romero to get along with the government, which the archbishop knew was killing his people.[12])

Days before their own deaths, Ita and Maura had flown to Nicaragua to attend a regional meeting of Maryknoll missionaries. At the closing liturgy for that gathering, on December 1, it was Ita who read aloud Romero's words: "Christ invites us not to fear persecution because, believe me, brothers and sisters, one who is committed to the poor must risk the same fate as the poor, and in El Salvador we know what the fate of the poor signifies: to disappear, to be tortured, to be captive, and to be found dead."[13] The next day, they flew back to El Salvador, where Dorothy and Jean met them at the airport and martyrdom met all four on the road.

Just as the martyrs of El Salvador offer us a modern model of courageous assent to God's call, and Mary's resounding yes to the Incarnation provided a paradigm of obedience, we look to Jesus himself for our sense of what is important and what is not. In his homily, John Paul asked Mary "to teach us the way of humble and joyful obedience to the Gospel in the service of our brothers and sisters, without preferences and without prejudices." Here, the pope cited the fourth chapter of Luke's Gospel, where Jesus describes his mission as a proclamation of good news to the poor, echoing the prophet Isaiah. For me, those verses in Luke are perhaps the most powerful in all of Scripture. They constitute, in effect, the inaugural address of Jesus, the program for his entire ministry.

> "When he came to Nazareth, where he had been brought up, he went to the synagogue on the sabbath day, as was his custom. He stood up to read, and the scroll of the prophet Isaiah was given to him. He unrolled the scroll and found the place where it was

written: 'The Spirit of the Lord is upon me, because he has anointed me to bring good news to the poor. He has sent me to proclaim release to the captives and recovery of sight to the blind, to let the oppressed go free, to proclaim the year of the Lord's favor.' And he rolled up the scroll, gave it back to the attendant, and sat down. The eyes of all in the synagogue were fixed on him. Then he began to say to them, 'Today this scripture has been fulfilled in your hearing.' "[14]

Every time I read this passage about Jesus preaching in the Nazareth synagogue, the hair on the back of my neck stands up. It provides a searing summary of what worries Jesus, what occupies his attention, what engages his passion. It's all about serving the poor and the marginalized, and not at all about sexual mores or ritual observance. That is not to say that ritual piety was totally unimportant to Jesus. He did, after all, pray in the synagogue "as was his custom." So he was not a three-times-a-year Jew, but a pious one. It is very easy to envision him wearing his prayer shawl in the prescribed manner as he held the scroll in his rough carpenter's hands and read out loud the words of Isaiah. But questions of ritual and of sexual mores, which occupy us so intensely, did not matter enough to him to make an appearance in this inaugural sermon. (Nor, for that matter, did they appear in Matthew 25, his terrifying forecast of how we will be sorted out at the final judgment, based on how we have fed and clothed the poor, welcomed the stranger and visited the sick and the imprisoned.[15]) Rather, he chose a verse that leads us directly to his heart, to his preoccupation with the poor and the powerless, the *anawim,* as Jesus would have known them.

Where did Jesus get this zeal for the poor? On his Father's side, it isn't difficult to figure out. The needs of the poor and the oppressed are among the most frequently mentioned themes in the Bible. They don't just appear in one or two verses, to be trotted out by a literalist to prove a minor point. The Bible is saturated with God's thirst for justice, and that is the note that Jesus, his son, sounds at the start of his ministry. I also like to think that Jesus learned some of his concern for the poor from his mother. Listen to this verse from Mary's song of joy when she visits Elizabeth: "He has brought down the powerful from their thrones, and lifted up the lowly; he has filled the hungry with good things, and sent the rich away empty."[16] It's true that most Scripture scholars agree that Mary did not spontaneously compose the Magnificat. In fact, Raymond Brown suggests that Luke got the text of this powerful canticle, just as he got the Benedictus of Zechariah, from early Jewish converts to Christianity who sold their worldly goods to feed the needy and became needy themselves, became *anawim*.[17] But Mary clearly embodies that piety of self-giving, of willing identification with the poor, and I cannot help but believe that Jesus learned some of it from her.

If we read all the way to the end of Luke's account of the inaugural sermon of Jesus, we learn something unsettling about ourselves, something powerful about prophetic speech. When Jesus finished reading from Isaiah in that little synagogue in Nazareth, his neighbors liked what they were hearing. "All spoke well of him and were amazed at the gracious words that came from his mouth."[18] But then Jesus went on to explain to them how a prophet is not honored in his own town and to give some examples of God's favor resting not on the Israelites, but on foreigners. That's when he lost them. "They got up, drove him out of the town, and took him to the brow of the hill on which the town was built, in order to throw him down the cliff. But he walked right through the crowd and went on his way."[19]

That's my idea of a homily: prophetic speech so profound that it moves its hearers to immediate action. Unfortunately, we do not experience it very often in our own lives. As Catholics, we have too often endured mumbled, ill-prepared, uninspired homilies, and they provoke nothing more than a languid yawn.

Perhaps that contrast is why this inaugural homily of Jesus in Nazareth always gets to me. Or perhaps it has something to do with my feeling that we too seldom remember that Jesus, our Lord, is also our great brother. (That phrase was the way Martin Buber, the eminent Jewish philosopher, described Jesus. In one of the odd twists of this trip, when Paul and I enjoyed a pleasant supper at Matt McAllester's Jerusalem apartment, we learned that Buber had once lived in it.)

Swept up in the divinity of Jesus, a belief that we all share as Christians, we lose sight of his glorious humanity. We focus so much on the Incarnation and the Resurrection, that we don't pay enough attention to what he said and did in the years between those two pivotal events. We accept salvation from his death, but we don't always draw lessons from his life. Almost 2,000 years after he stood before large and attentive gatherings in the vast outdoor classroom of Galilee, we still remember what he said, but we tend to take for granted what he was: an amazingly gifted teacher. We quote his words of comfort, but we remember too dimly that he was a fearless prophet, unafraid to speak the truth to power. We teach that Jesus had a threefold ministry, as priest, prophet and king, but we focus so much on priesthood and kingdom that we forget the costs of prophecy: the costs that he was willing to pay in his life, the costs that he asks to bear in ours, the price that Ita and Maura and Jean and Dorothy and Oscar paid without hesitation.

So Nazareth is the perfect place not only to reflect on Mary's courage at the Annunciation, but to recall the bravery of her son at the announcement of his program in the synagogue. In fact, just a short walk from the Basilica of the Annunciation is the Greek Catholic Synagogue Church, a simple stone structure from the Crusader era, believed to have been built on the site of the synagogue where Jesus preached. Typically, I didn't get to visit it, because I was rushing to get out of Nazareth, find transportation back to Jerusalem and write my part of the story.

If I had it all to do over again, I'd have awakened earlier, made a small pilgrimage to the Synagogue Church, and used the place to enrich my reflection on that sermon that still resonates for me two millennia after Jesus spoke the words.

Instead, moments after my interview with Joseph Khill, the choir director, I retrieved my overnight bag from my hotel and caught a cab to the press center at the Nazareth Marriott. The memory of the logistical nightmare of Friday afternoon was still painfully fresh, and the last thing I wanted was to find myself stranded in Nazareth, without transportation back to Jerusalem. In one of our cell-phone conversations, Paul had told me that Mark Matthews, the Jerusalem correspondent for our sister paper, *The Baltimore Sun*, would be heading back to Jerusalem, and that I might be able to get a ride from him. So I was determined to get to the press center before Mark left.

As I was about to get on the elevator from the hotel lobby to the press center, I ran into Moshe Milner, the photographer from the government press office who had rescued me the night before by giving me a ride to Nazareth. The moment he saw me, he asked: "Going to Jerusalem?" Those were among the three most welcome words I have ever heard. Not certain that I'd find Mark Matthews, I accepted Moshe's offer instantly. Minutes later, the two of us were on our way to Jerusalem.

That trip, a little less than two hours long, turned out to be a pleasant respite from the madness that I had experienced earlier in the week. For one thing, I had nothing to obsess about, because I'd be in Jerusalem in plenty of time to write. Also, Moshe was an excellent companion for the journey, filled with stories about past photographic assignments. Though he is Jewish, he knows a lot about the life of Jesus, because he had taken the photographs for a 1998 book called *Jesus 2000: A Walk with Jesus in the Holy Land*. At one point, he drew my attention to some lovely yellow flowering plants along the side of the road and mentioned that they are used to make mustard. Seeing them gave me a little chill, as I thought of the parable of the mustard seed.[20] Once again, being in the Holy Land, even on a modern road between Nazareth and Jerusalem, was heightening my ability to use my senses in meditating vividly on a Gospel text, as St. Ignatius Loyola prescribed centuries ago. The distance of the trip itself, two hours by car, gave me a sense of how long it would have taken Jesus to walk from his hometown to Jerusalem on foot. On the side of some hills as we neared the city, I saw markers for the elevation above sea level, and I gained a new appreciation for the way Jesus told his disciples about the fate awaiting him: "We are going up to Jerusalem. . . ."[21] Having covered the pope as he followed in the footsteps of Jesus to the baptismal site at the Wadi al-Kharrar, one of the lowest places on earth, I was now significantly above sea level as we neared Jerusalem. All of these little sensory markers, I realized, would forever enrich my reading of the Gospel.

Jerusalem: Gethsemane and the Greek Orthodox Patriarchate

The Prayer

In the Holy Land, where Christians live side by side with the followers of Judaism and Islam, where there are almost daily tensions and conflicts, it is essential to overcome the scandalous impression given by our disagreements and arguments. In this City it should be eminently possible for Christians, Jews and Muslims to live together in brotherhood and freedom, in dignity, justice and peace.

Reflection

Back In Jerusalem, I showered and joined Paul for a walk to the Old City. We tried to attend a Saturday evening Mass at St.

Saviour's Church, near the New Gate, but when we got there, we discovered that the Mass was in Arabic. Deciding to attend Mass on Sunday evening instead, we walked back to the hotel and wrote the story. Then we enjoyed a leisurely supper at the American Colony Hotel, where my long odyssey to the Sea of Galilee had begun two nights earlier in the rain.

Though our walk to the Old City had taken us close to the headquarters of the Greek Orthodox Patriarchate, neither of us had an invitation to be part of the press pool covering the pope's early-evening ecumenical speech there, following his visit to the Garden of Gethsemane, where Jesus prayed so intensely on the night before he died. The host for the ecumenical gathering was Diodoros I, the Greek Orthodox patriarch of Jerusalem. Before the pope's visit, there was ample reason to wonder how successful this meeting might be. Less than a month earlier, on the first-ever papal pilgrimage to Egypt, the pope had visited St. Catherine's, a monastery in the foothills of Mount Sinai, and encountered nettlesome reminders of the East-West split in Christianity dating back to the year 1054. The abbot, Archbishop Damianos, had addressed John Paul as "the president of the Roman Catholic Church," an oddly inaccurate title rooted in the harsh reality that the Orthodox do not recognize the primacy of the bishop of Rome. During his visit to the monastery, the pope prayed privately in the chapel. But Damianos did not join him in prayer, explaining later that it was against Orthodox canon law. Nor did the abbot hold out much hope for unity between Rome and the Orthodox.

Undaunted by the complications he had encountered at Mount Sinai, or by his continuing inability to realize his dream of visiting Russia, because the Russian Orthodox Church has never seen fit to invite him, John Paul gave a talk that recognized the obstacles but clung to a certain optimism. He addressed Diodoros respectfully as "Your Beatitude" and mused about the significance of this ecumenical moment.

"Need I say that I am greatly encouraged by this evening's meeting?" the pope asked. "It confirms that we have set out on the path to knowing one another better, with the desire to overcome the mistrust and rivalry inherited from the past. Here in Jerusalem, in the City where our Lord Jesus Christ died and rose from the dead, his words ring out with special resonance, particularly the words he spoke on the night before he died." John Paul cited the words from John's Gospel, "that they may all be one,"[22] that had inspired the title of his 1995 encyclical on Christian unity, *Ut Unum Sint*. "It is in response to that prayer of the Lord that we are together here, all followers of the one Lord despite our sad divisions, and all conscious that his will obliges us, and the Churches and Ecclesial Communities we represent, to walk the path of reconciliation and peace."

The phrase "ecclesial communities" is Vatican jargon. It drew increased attention in ecumenical circles not long after John Paul's pilgrimage to the Holy Land. On June 30, 2000, the Congregation for the Doctrine of the Faith, the Vatican's doctrinal guardian, issued a letter called *Note on the Expression "Sister Churches."* The document, apparently issued in reaction to what the Vatican saw as errors by some theologians, said that "the one, holy, catholic and apostolic universal church is not sister but *mother* of all the particular churches."[23] At a news conference on September 5, the Congregation for the Doctrine of the Faith dropped the other shoe, a longer document, dated August 6, called *Dominus Iesus: Declaration on the Unicity and Salvific Universality of Jesus Christ and the Church.* This document argued that "ecclesial communities which have not preserved the valid Episcopate and the genuine and integral substance of the Eucharistic mystery, are not Churches in the proper sense. . . ."[24] So, not long after John Paul used the term "ecclesial communities" at the patriarchate, it became even more distasteful to many non-Catholics, including the Orthodox. It is true that *Dominus Iesus* has far less weight than the papal encyclical on ecumenism, *Ut Unum Sint*, and less weight than the statements that John Paul wrote and delivered during his pilgrimage to the Holy Land. But that did not eliminate the disappointment that many non-Catholic Christian communities felt about the document.

Despite all the difficulties in Catholic-Orthodox relations, John Paul's talk at the patriarchate bravely pushed ahead, recalling an earlier meeting in Jerusalem in 1964 between his own predecessor, Pope Paul VI, and Ecumenical Patriarch Athenagoras I, the first among equals in the Orthodox world. "In the intervening years we have learned that the road to unity is a difficult one," the pope told the gathered Christian leaders. "This should not discourage us. We must be patient and persevering, and continue to move ahead without wavering. The warm embrace of Pope Paul and Patriarch Athenagoras stands out as a prophetic sign and source of inspiration, urging us on to new efforts to respond to the Lord's will."

In his talk, John Paul tried to strike a delicate balance between affirming the need for unity and rejoicing in the existing diversity. "The variety and beauty of your liturgical rites, and of your spiritual, theological and canonical traditions and institutions, testifies to the richness of the divinely revealed and undivided heritage of the universal Church, as it has developed down the centuries in the East and in the West," the pope said. "There exists a legitimate diversity which in no way is opposed to the unity of the Body of Christ, but rather enhances the splendor of the Church and contributes greatly to the fulfillment of her mission (cf. *Ut Unum Sint*, 50). None of this wealth must be lost in the fuller unity to which we aspire."

The language about unity and diversity could have appeared in any of John Paul's speeches on ecumenism, but this talk at the patriarchate offered him an opportunity that others could not: the grace of place, the ability to enrich the dialogue by rooting it in the unique location that is the focal point of all three major monotheistic faiths. "Only by being reconciled among themselves can Christians play their full part in making Jerusalem the City of Peace for all peoples," the pope said. "In the Holy Land, where Christians live side by side with the followers of Judaism and Islam, where there are almost daily tensions and conflicts, it is essential to overcome the scandalous impression given by our disagreements and arguments. In this City it should be eminently possible for Christians, Jews and Muslims to live together in brotherhood and freedom, in dignity, justice and peace."

Unfortunately, after John Paul and Diodoros had both spoken, the meeting displayed more division than unity. The leaders present could not even agree to recite in unison the Lord's Prayer, the prayer that Jesus himself prescribed. On one side of the room, Catholics and leaders of rites that recognize papal primacy rose and said the prayer in different languages, primarily Latin. On the other side, Orthodox leaders, including Diodoros himself, stood but did not pray aloud. (A few months later Diodoros died.)

This public inability to recite together the Lord's Prayer must have been a sad event for John Paul. In his writings, including the encyclical *Ut Unum Sint*, in his speeches, and in his public appearances for more than two decades, this pope has made it abundantly clear that Christian unity is a subject very close to his heart. But, as the documents that his doctrinal office issued later in the year made plain, the heart is not the only force that shapes the difficult struggle toward fuller Christian unity. The intellect also plays a central role, maintaining sharp edges in the hard debate over doctrine and truth, a debate that finds insurmountable stumbling blocks in such differences as the ordination of women, which the Catholic Church rejects and the Anglican Communion accepts, and the validity of all Anglican ordinations, which the Catholic Church denies.

On the same day that he ran into yet another evidence of the difficulties of seeking Christian unity, it seems fitting that John Paul also visited the Garden of Gethsemane, where Jesus prayed with such anguish on the eve of his own death. The night before he died, Jesus took with him only the tiny sub-committee of his closest followers: Peter, James and John. As they so often did, they disappointed him. This time, it was not a question of inability to understand, their most common fail-ing, but of insufficient perseverance. Repeatedly, in this moment of their master's great need, they fell asleep. Honestly, though, if we had been present that night, would we really have acted differently?

So much of the 2,000-year history of Christianity is a tale of followers too dense or too timid to imitate Jesus. For half of that time, those followers have been scattered, squabbling over the-ological niceties, just as the original apostles chose to pass too much of their time fussing over the best seats in the kingdom to come. Even today, with more ecumenical dialogues unfold-ing than ever before, the followers of Jesus are still disappoint-ing him. So, if the pope felt pain when other church leaders declined to pray the Lord's Prayer with him, that suffering seems a fitting echo of the suffering of Jesus at Gethsemane, where he prepared to offer his life for his friends, who down the centuries would choose to fight one another rather than uniting behind their self-emptying Lord. In that long and painful context, this evening in Jerusalem, when an aging pope spoke from the heart on the need for unity, will long be remem-bered as a historic and eloquent expression of both the yearn-ing and the hurt.

Questions for Reflection

1. Why does the lust for real estate, sacred or otherwise, always seem to frustrate the unifying and peacemaking dimen-sions of religious faith?

2. Besides his skills as a teacher, what other aspects of the glorious humanity of Jesus do we tend to forget?

3. Do we emulate the prophetic voice of Jesus? Are we willing to speak truth to power, no matter what the cost might be?

4. How do we deal with what we believe to be God's call to us? How do we discern what God is calling us to do in the specific circumstances of our lives?

5. What have we done to promote Christian unity?

6. Think of Jesus kneeling in agonized prayer in the Garden of Gethsemane the night before he died, and imagine him contemplating the failings of his followers through the millennia ahead of him. Which of our failings might have contributed to that pain?

Pope John Paul II kneels in prayer at an altar in the Church of the Holy Sepulchre, at the site of the Crucifixion.

Chapter 7

Sunday, March 26, 2000

Jerusalem: The Noble Sanctuary

In a moving finale to his seven days in the Holy Land, John Paul spent Sunday morning visiting the Haram al-Sharif, the third holiest place to Muslims; the Western Wall, holiest site for Jews; and the Church of the Holy Sepulchre, holiest place to Christians. He also met with local bishops at the Latin Rite patriarchate in the Christian Quarter of the Old City. Then, in a surprise, he later returned to the church to pray alone. After a farewell ceremony at Ben Gurion International Airport, he departed for Rome at 7 p.m. Paul wrote this chapter.

The Prayer

Jerusalem is the Holy City par excellence. It forms part of the common patrimony of our religions and of the whole of humanity. May the Almighty grant peace to the whole of this beloved region, so that all the people living in it may enjoy their rights, live in harmony and cooperation, and bear witness to the One God in acts of goodness and human solidarity. Thank you, all!

The Place

It's been called the earth's navel, the planet's true pole, the *Axis Mundi.* No place in the world compares to it: Haram al-Sharif, The Noble Sanctuary to Muslims and the Temple Mount to Jews. This is where Solomon built the Temple his father David envisioned, where a Second Temple was built in the sixth century B.C. after the Babylonians destroyed the first, and where King Herod erected a grand new complex that remained under construction in the time of Jesus, who prayed there. Lamented in the psalms, preached by the prophets, prayed

165

over by Jesus: It's simply an extraordinary place. Jewish legend holds it is where Abraham brought Isaac to be sacrificed. Muslims believe that the prophet Muhammad ascended to heaven from the same outcrop of rock after his night journey to Jerusalem. The Dome of the Rock, the gold-covered dome built over this rock, dominates the countryside. Completed in 691, its mathematically perfect proportions, immense inner space and intricate mosaics create a sense of awe in people of all faiths. The gold-lacquered dome, a beacon seen far and wide, points to heaven. Arches in front of the shrine are called the "scales," in accord with the Muslim belief that a balance will be hung there upon which human deeds will be weighed on Judgment Day.[1] The silver-domed al-Aqsa Mosque, located across the esplanade from the Dome of the Rock, was built in 715 and has been modified and rebuilt a number of times. Its carpeted interior is vast as a Roman basilica, with rows of marble columns setting off spaces for prayer. The windows admit so much light that the mosque seems to glow inside.

The immense, trapezoid-shaped platform Pope John Paul II visited as a guest of Muslim religious leaders was an engineering wonder when Herod created it. He widened the existing platform on which the 500-year-old Second Temple stood, filling in the hilltop and supporting it with 80-foot stone walls that had foundations reaching 50 feet below the surface. The stones used in these walls weighed as much as 100 tons each. The 172,000-square-yard platform and supporting walls survived the Romans' destruction of the Temple in 70.[2]

Beyond its huge significance for Judaism and Islam, the esplanade also has a tremendous resonance for Christians. A look at one Gospel, Luke, illuminates the Temple's importance in Jesus' life. Luke's account begins in the Temple sanctuary with the story of the priest Zechariah, father of John the Baptist. He is rendered mute when he refuses to believe the angel's declaration that his aging wife Elizabeth will have a son.

One might add that from the beginning of Christian literature, there is an ambivalence about the Temple. Compare the visits of two angels described at the start of Luke's Gospel. Zechariah, a priest, was overwhelmed by fear and did not accept God's word even as he stood beside the altar of incense in the Temple sanctuary. But when Mary, a young woman in a patriarchal society, was visited under much more humble circumstances far from the Temple in the hinterlands of Galilee, she overcame her doubt and told the angel, "Here am I, the servant of the Lord."[3] The difference is underscored by Zechariah's own wife, Elizabeth, when she greets the pregnant Mary: "Blessed is she who believed that there would be a fulfillment of what was spoken to her by the Lord."[4] Thus, God's plan for salvation was first greeted in a small town in Galilee and not in the holy sanctuary.

Nonetheless, Luke portrays the Temple as an important part of Jesus' life. As a child, he was presented there, in accordance with Mosaic law. Simeon recognized him as "a light for revelation to the Gentiles and for glory to your people Israel."[5] Jesus' parents found him at the age of 12 with the teachers in the Temple after he'd been missing for three days.[6] Later in his life, he returned to clear the Temple of vendors and to teach there himself.[7] The Temple continues to be mentioned in the Acts of the Apostles, which the author of Luke wrote. Peter heals a cripple beside a gate to the Temple and addresses the Jewish people from Solomon's Portico, where the disciples gathered.[8]

With so many references to the Temple in the New Testament, the Haram al-Sharif takes on immense meaning for Christian visitors in addition to their appreciation for its role in Islam and Judaism. I found it a beautiful spot in which to linger and view the countryside—the Mount of Olives, the Kidron Valley, the distant hills—from an important place in Jesus' life. The pine trees, the bells chiming in the city, the mottled stone paths, the graceful domes, small and large, that dot the esplanade: All this builds a feeling of peace, a sense of what was and hope for what will be. It is a place to reflect, to dwell on Christianity's debt to Judaism and also to appreciate the Muslims' deep expression of faith in the One God.

Reflection

History weighed most heavily on John Paul's stooped shoulders as he began the dramatic final day of his Holy Land pilgrimage with a morning visit to The Noble Sanctuary. Despite—or perhaps, because of—its holiness to the three major monotheistic faiths, it is ground zero for contemporary political strife in the Middle East; the unending battle to control the site is the largest obstacle to peace in the region. During John Paul's visit, these tensions mingled with the holy site's sad history, catapulting the past into the present. With the pope's white robes resplendent under the clear blue sky and the Muslim clerics wearing turbans, their meeting in front of the 1,300-year-old Dome of the Rock looked almost like a gathering that could have occurred centuries ago (if one could ignore the white Chevrolet Suburban that transported John Paul through the Old City that day).

In my visit a few days earlier, I lingered on the esplanade, absorbing a place where the deep recesses of the past are infused into the present, where long-term memory is as sharp as the recall of last week's headlines. That sense of merging past and present tense returned in what struck me as the most telling moment of John Paul's complex visit to this holy place. It came as he left a meeting with Muslim clerics, amid pushing and shoving between Palestinian security guards and about fifteen Palestinian demonstrators. "Shame on you!" one of the demonstrators yelled at the Palestinian authorities. "Saladin took the keys; now you have handed them over to the pope."

Saladin was the Muslim warrior who peacefully conquered Jerusalem from the Crusaders on October 2, 1187, the day Muslims celebrate Muhammad's night journey to Jerusalem.

(This was not the first time his name had come up during John Paul's pilgrimage; the mosque at the center of controversy in Nazareth was to be built on the burial site of Saladin's nephew, adjacent to the Basilica of the Annunciation.) Saladin refrained from avenging the Crusaders' 1099 conquest, in which the Christians had massacred 10,000 Muslims who sought safety at their Noble Sanctuary, an attack that gave new meaning to the lament of Psalm 79: "They have poured out their blood like water all around Jerusalem." The Christian army, of course, had been dispatched by one of John Paul's predecessors, Pope Urban II, who ordered the first Crusade to cheers that "God wills it" and incited military leaders with anti-Muslim propaganda.[9] It took Saladin to show the Crusaders what it meant to be Christian.

It's a safe guess that none of the local people present the day of John Paul's visit would have to look this up in a history book.

Against that historical background—perhaps one should say historical foreground in this case—John Paul's simple presence once again made a powerful statement. There was the pope, the brilliant gold dome so holy to Muslims towering over his head, the intricate blue and gold mosaic his backdrop. Through his presence, he recognized the importance of this holy place to Muslims, countering a sad and very present past.

Perhaps the best thing that could have happened after his arrival would have been for everyone to spontaneously pray in silence to the One God and to reflect on the wonder of the moment, but that was not to be. Instead, after a series of hospitable introductions, the conversation on the esplanade took a political turn when John Paul found himself facing a white-bearded sheikh who shook his finger in the pontiff's face and urged that he raise his voice against "all the people who destroyed the houses and who put my people inside the prison." It was startling to see the pope harangued, given the care taken to assure a dignified atmosphere at his public appearances. But as bad as it looked, the sheikh was not criticizing the pope; he was asking his help. John Paul seemed to accept it with equanimity as he slowly moved toward an office where Grand Mufti Ekrima Sa'id Sabri would host a formal meeting.

The political jockeying was intense that morning, with Israeli police preventing Palestinian flags from being raised during the papal visit and stopping an attempt by right-wing Jews to fly an Israeli flag attached to a helium balloon. At the Haram, Palestinians were edgy because of the Israeli security present for the papal visit. As the pope entered the compound, hundreds of balloons in the Palestinian flag's colors of green, red and black were released into the air while a thousand schoolchildren chanted, "Long live Palestine!"[10]

This gamesmanship to assert sovereignty over The Temple Mount/Noble Sanctuary would seem almost childish if there were not so much at stake. Consider the events that occurred there just six months after the pope's visit when Ariel Sharon, a hardnosed Israeli politician, who less than a year later was elected prime minister, insisted on visiting the area with a large security force to assert Israeli control. Demonstrations begat rioting in which four people were killed, which led to armed confrontations in which hundreds died, thousands were injured and the whole Middle East was thrown into turmoil. It's no wonder that the Gospel of Luke records Jesus weeping at the sight of Jerusalem.

The meeting with John Paul was cordial, with the Muslim hosts seeming to clearly enjoy the pope's presence. Sabri, speaking in Arabic, sat to one side of the pontiff while Latin Rite Patriarch Michel Sabbah, seated to John Paul's right, translated. Among those to welcome the pope was a smiling Sheikh Taysir Tamimi, the cleric who had left the pope's interreligious meeting at Notre Dame Center three days before.

Politics, so fused with religion in the Middle East, continued to hover over the event as the grand mufti spoke of how

Jerusalem was "eternally bonded to Islam" because of Muhammad's miraculous night journey there. He sought the pope's help "to end the Israeli occupation of Jerusalem" and spoke of how it was difficult for Muslim worshipers to reach the holy place because of "the tight military siege" around the city. (A short time later, in a separate ceremony before the Western Wall, an Israeli cabinet minister, Rabbi Michael Melchior, declared that Jerusalem was "our eternal homeland and capital.")

John Paul began his brief remarks by finding common ground at the holy place for "all believers," which would have to mean not only Muslims and Christians but Jews as well. He thanked Sabri "for receiving me within the Haram al-Sharif, which is connected with the memory of Abraham, who for all believers is a model of faith and submission to Almighty God."

John Paul once again deflected political discourse, turning it aside as gently as he might an intruding thought during his meditation. "This visit of mine, as you are aware, is essentially a religious and spiritual pilgrimage," he said. "Pilgrimage to holy places is a feature common to many religious traditions, especially to the three Abrahamic religions. . . . Jerusalem is the Holy City par excellence. It forms part of the common patrimony of our religions and of the whole of humanity."

His message was gentle but quite clear: John Paul had not come to take sides in the dispute between Muslims and Jews over this holy place. Jerusalem, he told his hosts, was for all humankind. "May the Almighty grant peace to the whole of this beloved region, so that all the people living in it may enjoy their rights, live in harmony and cooperation, and bear witness to the One God in acts of goodness and human solidarity," he prayed, adding, "Thank you, all!"

Ideally, a visitor to the holy esplanade should be able to screen out the political distractions like so many souvenir sellers and would-be tour guides. For Americans, especially, there is a tradition of separating religion and politics. But Jerusalem teaches otherwise—that it's not so easy to separate the two.

The grand mufti was unapologetic about this. "We can't divide the political part of the religion," he said to the reporters who visited his home several days before the pope's arrival in the Holy Land. "They are together." Underscoring this, the mufti had a painting on his living room's wall that depicted a man pulling to shore a boat carrying Jerusalem, the Dome of the Rock predominating. It was slowly gaining ground on the shore, the mufti explained, but had "not yet" landed. The painting signified that Muslims were slowly and laboriously bringing Jerusalem into their harbor.

In Muslim eyes, the West similarly mixes religion and politics but denies doing so. In the nineteenth century—which in the Old City seems scarcely more than the day before yesterday—Pope Pius IX, under siege and facing the loss of the papal states, condemned religious tolerance and the separation of church and state, insisting that Catholicism get special government treatment. (John Paul beatified him several months after his pilgrimage in the Holy Land, an action considered in the Jewish community to be a disturbing sign for Catholic-Jewish relations because of what was seen as Pius' hostility to the Jews of his day.)

It doesn't work for outsiders to come to Jerusalem and try to superimpose their political traditions on the struggles there. In the end, many of the traditions of Jerusalem are our traditions, more deeply rooted than we know. Religion and politics have been entwined for a long time and they don't separate easily, even in American culture. John Paul offered, then, a solution for handling this inflammatory mixture. His answer is not to run away from faith when dealing with political matters but rather to be true to the heart of religious traditions: to "bear witness to the One God in acts of goodness and human solidarity."

Jerusalem: The Western Wall

The Prayer

God of our fathers, you chose Abraham and his descendants to bring your name to the nations: We are deeply saddened by the behavior of those who in the course of history have caused these children of yours to suffer, and asking your forgiveness, we wish to commit ourselves to genuine brotherhood with the people of the covenant.

The Place

"If I forget you, O Jerusalem, let my right hand wither!" the psalmist wrote. "May my tongue cling to the roof of my mouth, if I do not remember you, if I do not set Jerusalem above my highest joy."[11] The Western Wall is where the Jewish people remember who they are and who God made them to be. It is the surviving remnant of the Temple the Romans destroyed, a retaining wall King Herod built in 20 B.C. With rock plants sinking their roots into crevices between the massive chunks of limestone, it is a symbol of the Jewish people and their resilience against centuries of persecution. This is where all prayers from the world over rise to God, according to a Jewish tradition, the place from which God's presence never budges.

As the authors of this book found, the Wall is a powerful place for anyone to pray. You feel as if God is looking right through you. Visiting the Wall is like seeing a deceased loved one in a very vivid dream—it calls out to be touched, to be kissed, to be cried over. It is past and present folded into the same moment. Custom calls for writing a prayer on a small piece of paper and folding it into a crevice—fulfilling the need one feels for a visible way of talking to God, whose presence feels so strong.

The Ottoman ruler Sultan Suleiman the Magnificent gave permission in the sixteenth century for Jews to have a place of prayer at the Western Wall. Jews who prayed there would break down into tears as they remembered their people's losses, leading to the name "Wailing Wall," which still appears on some directional signs in the Old City. Within several decades, it became clear that having both Muslims and Jews worship in close proximity raised tensions.[12] For one thing, Arabs' homes were built close to the Wall, a situation that lasted until Israel seized the area from Jordan in 1967 during the Six Day War. Soon after, the homes were demolished, creating a broad plaza that seems all the more immense, given the Old City's claustrophobia-inducing narrow, winding streets.

To reach the Wall, visitors must pass through a security gate; men whose heads are not covered must don a *kippah*, or skullcap. (Bob, loyal fan, wore his New York Mets hat.) The area is divided into two sections, one for men and the other for women. The Wall is lit at night and visitors can go there around the clock.

In addition to reflecting on their roots in Judaism, Christians can also appreciate this as a place Jesus knew, masonry that once held up the building he cherished as "my Father's house."[13]

Reflection

Michael Melchior's voice boomed across the expanse of the Western Wall plaza, inviting John Paul and millions of television viewers around the world to grasp the history behind a historic moment. "Your Honor, the Pope," Israel's minister of diaspora affairs began. "Thousands of years of history are looking down on us from atop this sacred mount and from amidst the stones of the remnant of our holy Temple." He added: "And they see you here." In a voice at once gracious and insistent, Melchior explained to the pontiff why the eyes of history were upon him: "We welcome your coming here as the realization of the commitment of the Catholic Church to end the era of hatred, humiliation and persecution of the Jewish people."

There was no doubt about it: Pope John Paul II carried the burden of history that day, first from the Muslim sanctuary and now to the Western Wall. As Melchior indicated, it was a heavy load. Through the centuries, the Catholic Church had legislated against the Jews in many ways, prohibiting them from marrying Christians or holding public office, among other measures. These prohibitions paled before the pogroms of the Crusaders, who slaughtered Jews in France, Germany and Bohemia on their way to the Holy Land. When they conquered Jerusalem in 1099, the Crusaders rounded up Jews into a synagogue and murdered them. In 1215, the Fourth Lateran Council required Jews 12 years and older to wear distinctive clothing—badges. It also barred Jews from appearing in public during Easter week; required Jews to pay a tithe on their property to the church at Easter; and threatened excommunication for Christian princes who appointed a Jew to public office. Pope Paul IV ordered the Jews of Rome to live in a ghetto in 1555. In other words, the anti-Semitism prevalent in Christian society was not simply a matter of individual Christians misunderstanding their faith. The Church's magisterium, through synods, councils and warfare that the popes initiated, was also responsible. Apologists have argued that Church leaders who encouraged forced conversions and other restrictions on the Jews were responding in good faith, conditioned by historical circumstance. But this argument is undercut by the fact that over the centuries, a number of popes with a clear understanding of the Christian message did try to protect the Jews.

Into the twentieth century, the Catholic Church continued to explain away this shameful history. It is chilling to read the 1910 edition of *The Catholic Encyclopedia*, which defends the church's history of anti-Jewish laws:

"The obligation of wearing a distinguishing badge was of course obnoxious to the Jews. At the same time, Church authorities deemed its injunction necessary to prevent effectively moral offenses between Jews and Christian women. The decrees forbidding the Jews from appearing in public at Eastertide may be justified on the ground that some of them mocked at the Christian processions at that time."

The encyclopedia goes so far as to state: "It was for the laudable reason of protecting social morality and securing the maintenance of the Christian Faith, that canonical decrees were framed and repeatedly enforced against free and constant intercourse between Christians and Jews, against, for instance, bathing, living, etc., with Jews. To some extent, likewise, these were the reasons for the institution of the Ghetto or confinement of the Jews to a special quarter, for the prohibition of the Jews from exercising medicine, or other professions."[14]

It's startling to see that the encyclopedia, published with ecclesiastical approval, goes on to explain the "more or less justified" reasons for the popular hatred of the Jews, including the "patriotic susceptibilities of the particular nations in the midst of which the Jews have usually formed a foreign element, and to the respective interests of which their devotion has not always been beyond suspicion."

The remarks reflect a tradition of apologetics in which the Church refused to acknowledge any shortcoming whatsoever. Seen with the Holocaust in hindsight, it looks not merely triumphalistic but frightening. Many measures created by the medieval church would be adopted by the Nazis, who began their assault on the Jewish people with restrictions on intermarriage, travel and work, as well as the requirement that Jews wear identifying badges. Gradually tightening their grasp, the Nazis then forced Jews into disease-ridden ghettoes, and finally, set out on the "Final Solution," elimination. (The exhibits at Yad Vashem are very effective in showing how the executioner's noose gradually tightened.) As theologian Hans Küng has written, "Nazi anti-semitism, however much it may have been primarily the work of godless and criminal men, would have been impossible without the pre-ceding two thousand years of 'Christian' hostility to the Jews, which hampered Christians in offering convinced and ener-getic resistance to it on a broad front."[15]

The Church changed course in 1965 when the Second Vatican Council issued the landmark document called *Nostra Aetate*, "The Declaration on the Relationship of the Church to Non-Christian Religions." It specifically repudiated the idea that the Jewish people were responsible for the crucifixion of Jesus and rejected discrimination based on religion.

And so, the eloquent Michael Melchior declared, John Paul's visit brought a beginning after the end of centuries of persecu-tion: "For today begins a new era, in which we all lift our eyes to the heavens and commit ourselves to search every ancient path and to pave bold, new highways that will bring peace to all religions and to all believers—Jews, Christians and Moslems." As Melchior said, many would be watching—and history would judge—how he handled this golden moment at the Western Wall.

Head tilted to one side, the pope listened to the speech. The mood was uplifting: The broad open plaza contrasted with the narrow streets of the Old City and the brilliant sunshine was a welcome change from a week that had been largely overcast and cool. Then John Paul prayed Psalm 122 in Latin, beginning: "I was glad when they said to me, 'Let us go to the house of the Lord!' Our feet are standing within your gates, O Jerusalem." It's one of the psalms of ascent, the songs pilgrims would sing as they traveled the road up to Jerusalem's heights. In Psalm 122, the pilgrim has joyfully arrived in the Holy City, its walls offering refuge after a dangerous trip: "Peace be within your walls and security within your towers." It is the prayer of every pilgrim, in Biblical times and now, to be able to visit the holy places in security and peace.

After Melchior prayed the psalm in Hebrew, John Paul began a long, slow walk across the plaza to the Western Wall, using his cane. His halting approach heightened the solemnity and sense of significance in having the bishop of Rome arrive as a pilgrim at the place holiest to Jews. He was plunging into a mystery, the mystery of God's presence and of God's choice of the Jewish people as his own. And like a diver plunging deeper into the sea toward a sunken treasure, the pressure on him seemed to grow the further he went, the weight of history accumulating like pounds of water per square inch.

John Paul bowed in silence, blessed the Wall, then grasped a stone block with his shaking left hand, murmuring in prayer. It was a powerful image, the aged pope before the ancient Wall, the spiritual leader of Roman Catholicism showing reverence for the place holiest to a people Christians had persecuted for so long. Before turning to leave, John Paul slipped a note against the stones:

God of our fathers
you chose Abraham and his descendants
to bring your Name to the Nations:
we are deeply saddened
by the behavior of those
who in the course of history
have caused these children of yours to suffer,
and asking your forgiveness
we wish to commit ourselves
to genuine brotherhood
with the people of the Covenant.

Jerusalem, 26 March 2000
Joannes Paulus II

He turned away and then looked back to pray once more before departing.

The note, quickly taken to the Holocaust museum at Yad Vashem, revealed John Paul's intentions: He had come to ask forgiveness. These were the same words he had read during the prayer of the faithful in the dramatic "Day of Pardon" Mass celebrated at St. Peter's Basilica two Sundays earlier—but the setting was so different. At St. Peter's, he'd been surrounded by cardinals, by pomp and power in the majestic baroque basilica. But in Jerusalem, he stood alone before a stone wall, a sojourner seeking forgiveness.

John Paul had been hoping to make a sweeping gesture; initially, he wanted to reconcile with Jerusalem's chief rabbis at the Wall. (They preferred to meet with him in their ceremonial residence, a gesture of respect Rabbi Lau said Pope Paul VI declined to make in his 1964 visit.) But the pope had found the symbolism to make a powerful statement that will resonate long through the history of Catholic-Jewish relations. Because of the setting, it was an emotional moment for Israelis who watched either from the plaza or through live television broadcasts. Even the few reporters lucky enough to be in the small pool that provided coverage came back to the press center (where I watched via a video feed) with eyes bright and wide; they had seen something special.

Every reporter on the story knew that the picture of John Paul leaving a note at the Western Wall was a historic image that would be on the front page of newspapers around the world. But as moving as the image is, I think that in some ways, it doesn't tell the full story. We see a picture of one solitary man in a place where many can usually be found at prayer, suggesting that the pope alone is shouldering the weight of history. His goal, though, was for all Christians to join him. Throughout his pilgrimage, John Paul hoped that his fellow Christians would follow along in his footsteps. This was especially true when he sought God's forgiveness for the sins of all Christians, past and present. As he once remarked to reporters on a papal trip, "Why is it that it is only the pope who must apologize?"[16]

John Paul had indeed come to see the wounds of the Jewish people and to salve them—but no less so to heal the wounds afflicting his own flock. The whole church, the pope has written, should seek "the purification of memory," which he said "calls *everyone* to make an act of courage and humility in recognizing the wrongs done by those who have borne or bear the name of Christian."[17]

For John Paul, repentance and forgiveness were the key to the Jubilee Year celebration, the doorway to joy. "Acknowledging the weaknesses of the past is an act of honesty and courage which helps us to strengthen our faith, which alerts us to face today's temptations and challenges and prepares us to meet them,"[18] he wrote in *Tertio Millennio Adveniente*. John Paul's visit to the Western Wall was as much about the present as the past, an effort to strengthen the faith of the church today by relieving it of yesterday's burdens.

The pope encountered some criticism in Israel for not admitting wrongdoing on the part of the institutional Church or apologizing for what some charged was the Church's inaction during the Holocaust—he always spoke instead of Church members' sins. But in his writings, he has used the image of the Church as the Mystical Body of Christ—all members, living and dead, united in one Body with Christ as the head—to explain the need for all to acknowledge the sins of the past.

"Because of the bond which unites us to one another in the Mystical Body, all of us, though not personally responsible . . . bear the burden of the errors and faults of those who have gone before us,"[19] he wrote in explaining the need to seek forgiveness in the Jubilee Year. He said that "in this year of mercy the Church . . . should kneel before God and implore forgiveness for the past and present sins of her sons and daughters." By "the Church," John Paul meant the entire Body—including those of us watching him on television that Sunday morning at the Western Wall in Jerusalem.

We all carry the weight of history.

Jerusalem: Church of the Holy Sepulchre

The Prayers

At the dawn of a new Millennium, there is a great need to proclaim from the rooftops the Good News that "God so loved the world that he gave his only Son, that whoever believes in him should not perish, but have eternal life." (John 3:16). "Lord, you have the words of eternal life." (John 6:68). Today, as the unworthy Successor of Peter, I wish to repeat these words as we celebrate the Eucharistic Sacrifice in this, the most hallowed place on earth. With all of redeemed humanity, I make my own the words which Peter the Fisherman spoke to the Christ, the Son of the living God: "Lord, to whom shall we go? You have the words of eternal life."

Christos anesti.

Jesus Christ is risen! He is truly risen! Amen.

Angelus

In contemplating the Theotokos, almost at this journey's end, we look upon the true face of the Church, radiant in all her beauty. . . . O Advocate, help the Church to be ever more like you, her exalted model. Help her to grow in faith, hope and love, as she searches out and does the will of God in all things. O clement, O loving, O sweet Virgin Mary!

The Place

The Church of the Holy Sepulchre is built over the place where Jesus was crucified and buried. While experts dispute the authenticity of many ancient holy places, there is a consensus among Biblical archaeologists and New Testament scholars

that this is indeed the location of the final events in Jesus' life.[20]
This knowledge makes a visit to the holiest place in
Christendom all the more powerful; it is the location of
Golgotha, the skull-shaped rocky outcrop where Jesus was crucified just outside the city walls. Nowadays, it is well within the
Old City's walls, a fact that raised doubts in the nineteenth century when an alternate burial site, still called the Garden Tomb,
was discovered elsewhere in Jerusalem. Further research has
shown the Garden Tomb is not Jesus' burial place; in the 1960s,
British archaeologist Kathleen Kenyon was able to demonstrate
that the Church of the Holy Sepulchre was built beside a for-
mer stone quarry that would have been outside the city walls
at the time of the crucifixion. The Emperor Hadrian filled in the
quarry in 135 and built a temple as part of his plan to turn
Jerusalem into a Roman city, punishment against the Jews for
revolting. When the Emperor Constantine converted to
Christianity in the fourth century, he ordered the temple
destroyed and began an excavation to prepare construction of
the church. The tradition that Golgotha and the burial place lay
beneath the temple must have been very strong because it
would have been cheaper for Constantine to build his new
church in honor of Jesus' resurrection on an adjacent open area.
In his *Life of Constantine*, Eusebius wrote:

> "The Emperor . . . commanded that the stone and
> timber of the ruins should be removed and dumped as
> far away as possible, and that a large area of the foun-
> dation soil, defiled as it was by devil-worship, should
> be dug away to a depth, and removed to some distance.
>
> "At once the work was carried out, and, as layer
> after layer of the subsoil came into view, the venerable
> and most holy memorial of the Savior's resurrection,
> beyond all our hopes, came into view; the holy of
> holies, the considerable Cave, was, like our Savior,
> 'restored to life' . . . by its very existence being clearer

testimony to the resurrection of the Savior than any words."[21]

The visitor hoping to experience the same sense of wonder faces some serious obstacles. For starters, invaders destroyed the tomb unearthed in Eusebius' day; various replicas have replaced it over the years. The splendor of the church Constantine built is long gone; invaders destroyed it in 614 and 1009. The Crusaders restored and substantially changed it in the twelfth century, putting up one large building over the two that were on the site, but the church was damaged by fire in 1808 and an earthquake in 1927.

We are left with a "dark and dreary" church (as a priest described it in his homily at Mass there the morning after the papal visit) in need of renovation—a difficult task because of the long-standing quarrels among the churches sharing juris-diction over the building. The Armenian, Greek Orthodox and Roman Catholic churches have rights protected by the "status quo" reached in 1878 as part of the Treaty of Berlin, with the Coptic, Ethiopian and Syrian Orthodox holding small areas as well. It reverts to earlier treaties that Catholics involved in these matters feel to this day gave their interests short shrift. The treaty settled a dispute over the holy places that was the imme-diate cause of the Crimean War, which was fought from 1853 to 1856 between Russia on one side and France, England, the Ottoman empire and Sardinia on the other. The bloody fighting and mistreatment of the wounded soldiers led to the work of Florence Nightingale. (Given this rather recent history, Christians certainly do not have the right to feel superior to Muslims and Jews for battling over the Temple Mount/Haram al-Sharif.)

After the treaty, the churches settled into a sort of cold war, constantly guarding their turf against the others. Despite such vigilant monitoring, the atmosphere in this holy place is often anything but holy: Restless travelers line up at the tomb with all the decorum, at times, of tourists waiting for the elevator to the top of the Empire State Building. It is noisy, crowded and, with its profusion of chapels and passageways, confusing.

I was taken aback by this atmosphere in my first visit to the church in 1992, when I was shadowed by people who wanted to change money or be hired as a guide. But when I got the chance to sit quietly before a mosaic of Jesus being nailed to the cross, which overhangs an altar built atop Calvary, I found myself in tears while reading the Passion according to Matthew. Religion is communicated best in stories and the story of the Crucifixion is the most powerful of all, ingrained in mind, heart and soul. Mark Twain captured the essence of a visit to this church in his 1869 book *Innocents Abroad*: "With all its clap-trap side-shows and unseemly impostures of every kind, it is still grand, reverend, venerable—for a god died there; for fifteen hundred years its shrines have been wet with the tears of pilgrims from the earth's remotest confines." Twain, who poked fun at some of the historical claims made for sites in the Holy Land, was very serious about standing atop the rock of Calvary. "I climbed the stairway in the church which brings one to the top of the small inclosed pinnacle of rock, and looked upon the place where the true cross once stood, with a far more absorbing interest than I had ever felt in any thing earthly before," he wrote.

No other church, however intricate its stained glass, graceful its spires or massive its dome, captures the mysteries of Christianity the way this one does. Pilgrims can lose themselves amid a mélange of passageways and stairways leading to, among other things, Jewish tombs from the first century, a chapel with a portal through which one can touch the actual rock of Calvary, an ornate pillar thought to mark the center of the world, and an underground route, marked with ancient graffiti, leading to the cave where it is said Constantine's mother, Helena, discovered the True Cross. I found myself returning there as often as I had time, each visit yielding new shades of meaning. It is "the Mother of All Churches," as John Paul said, quoting St. John Damascene.

The pope arrived there behind an entourage of four *kawas*, fez-wearing escorts who clear a path for distinguished guests through the crowded streets of the Old City by pounding ominous-looking canes to the stone pavement. The church, unlike many of the world's famous cathedrals, doesn't stand out from the landscape: Jerusalem is too crowded to offer such vistas. Instead, one comes upon the small square in front of the church almost as a surprise. The Muslim keeper of the keys greeted John Paul—because of infighting among Christians, the task of opening and closing the church each day is assigned to Muslims—and the pontiff proceeded down a wooded ramp built earlier in the week to bridge the steps. Once inside the entrance, he bypassed a steep, winding stairway immediately to the right that climbs up to Greek Orthodox and Catholic chapels built over the rock of Calvary in a sort of medieval split-level fashion, between the floor and ceiling. Instead, he walked straight ahead to the long, flat stone of unction, placed on the site where tradition holds that Jesus' body was anointed after his death. He knelt, with some help, and kissed the stone, bending low. After welcoming speeches, he blessed those present, then turned and walked to the large rotunda built over the tomb.

The rotunda's ceiling gleamed with twelve golden rays against a mother of pearl background, representing the apostles; each ray had three more golden streams, signifying the Trinity. The ceiling was restored in 1997, a huge achievement given the centuries of battling among the Christian faiths to control the sacred building. Above the tomb was a nineteenth-century edicule often ridiculed as an eyesore, a grandiose mausoleum surrounded by hanging lanterns. To sounds of the *Te Deum*, the pope bowed to enter the low entrance, stopping first in an outer room where he lit a candle. Then he crouched to pass through another portal to the tomb, where he knelt, put both hands to the slab of marble and, in a solemn moment, kissed a stone burnished smooth by the lips of so many pilgrims.

Reflection

In his homily, the pope referred to the church by its Greek name, *Anastasis*, or Resurrection. Many consider this the better name for the church because ideally, it is a place to experience Christ's never-ending resurrection. If a visit there is to be something more than a museum trip, the pilgrim needs to come away with a sense of the risen Christ's enduring presence. That presence is celebrated in every Mass, everywhere. But I found that the empty tomb's proximity provided a new perspective on the Mass' summit, the sharing of bread and wine transformed into the body and blood of Christ. At Mass the morning after the pope departed, the celebrant prepared the Eucharist inside the tomb. It seemed almost comic to me at first, as if the priest had gone backstage. With his voice muffled, it sounded as if he were calling from the bottom of a well. But when he emerged nimbly from the tomb and held aloft the consecrated host before the congregation, there was a magical moment: The Eucharist is the Risen Christ. I've never seen a better explanation.

The solemn Mass John Paul celebrated before a small altar placed in front of the tomb's entrance also exuded the Resurrection. Putting aside centuries of resentment and bitterness among their churches, leaders from many faiths were present for the ceremony, which presented a visual feast of religious garb. There were the pointed hats of the Armenians, the rounded headgear worn by the Coptic and Syrian Orthodox leaders, the fluffy white beards, staffs of many kinds, encrusted with mosaics and silver, a multitude of hanging lamps. The pope wore purple vestments for Mass of the third Sunday in Lent. The sense of mingling and even unity grew as candles were lit from a flame inside the tomb, the ancient *lucernarium*. The same ceremony is described in *Egeria's Travels*, the account of a pilgrim who visited the church late in the fourth century. She reported that the ritual was enacted each day at the tomb: "The lamps and candles are all lit, which makes it very bright. The fire is brought not from outside, but from the cave—inside the screen—where a lamp is always burning night and day."[22]

Each person held a candle, the light creating a glow in the rotunda's stony confines, suggesting a warmth that is so often lacking among the competing churches (but, it should be noted, is often found among ordinary Christians in the Holy Land, who have a sense of solidarity). A day earlier, an attempt to pray the Our Father had only highlighted the Orthodox-Catholic division. But here, in the place where Jesus rose from the dead, there was a sense that Christ was rising in the Christian church.

Consider how uplifting and refreshing John Paul's visit was against the background of pettiness and bickering that tarnishes the history of this building. He brought a sense of optimism and unity so powerful that, like the candlelight symbolic of the risen Christ's presence, it overrode the darkness of centuries of misunderstanding.

His homily was a song of praise "to the central event of human history," the Resurrection of Jesus Christ. His journey through the history of salvation—from the peak of Mount Nebo, where Moses viewed the Promised Land; to Bethlehem, Nazareth and Galilee; to the Jordan River, the Upper Room and Gethsemane—had now climaxed beside the empty tomb. The pope's message "in this, the most hallowed place on earth," was intensely optimistic and humanistic.

"The Resurrection of Jesus is the definitive seal of all God's promises, the birth place of a new, risen humanity," he said in his homily. " . . . At the dawn of a new millennium, Christians can and ought to look to the future with steadfast trust in the glorious power of the Risen One to make all things new."

So the Resurrection never ends: It continues to renew, to rise within us, and can help us overcome divisions in everyday life and even, the pope implied, the kind of long-term bitterness found in the Holy Land. "Here at the Holy Sepulchre and Golgotha, as we renew our profession of faith in the Risen Lord, can we doubt that in the power of the Spirit of Life we will be given the strength to overcome our divisions and to work together to build a future of reconciliation, unity and peace?" John Paul declared. "Here, as in no other place on earth, we hear the Lord say once again to his disciples, 'Do not fear, I have overcome the world!' "

As occurred so often during John Paul's pilgrimage to the Holy Land, the visual image of the event spoke at least as powerfully as his words. In this case, the leaders of churches that had fought bitterly for centuries were gathered amicably, sharing the light, as millions of people watched on television. It seemed to be visible proof of the pope's end-of-millennium faith that ancient divisions—even "scandalous" ones, as he had called the break between the Eastern and Western churches one day earlier—could be healed with God's help.

A solemn note entered the pope's homily at that point as he said that in the Resurrection, Jesus "opens the way to the great Sabbath rest, the Eighth Day, when mankind's pilgrimage will come to its end and God will be all in all." John Paul's own pilgrimage was drawing to an end, both his seven-day visit to the Holy Land, and in another sense, his lifelong journey to seek God. But sitting there, faced toward the entrance of the empty tomb, he saw no reason for pessimism at that late juncture. "Today, as the unworthy Successor of Peter, I wish to repeat these words," he said, quoting Peter's words to Jesus. " 'Lord, to whom shall we go? You have the words of eternal life.' "

The end of his pilgrimage was not an end at all. His explanation: "*Christos anesti.* Jesus Christ is risen! He is truly risen!"

In those last hours of his pilgrimage, John Paul allowed a small window into his inner self. His remarks about the Eighth

Day were a reflection on his own mortality—and by extension, on the mortality of all the pope's pilgrims. Me. You. Before Mass ended in the Church of the Holy Sepulchre, he reflected once again in remarks that preceded the Angelus, a prayer of devotion to Mary. In one sentence, he captured the deep feelings that resonated throughout his pilgrimage:

"These have indeed been days of intense emotion, a time when our soul has been stirred not only by the memory of what God has done but by his very presence, walking with us once again in the Land of Christ's birth, death and resurrection."

For me, it was one of the pope's key quotes, a summary of the entire trip. I put it right near the top of the story I wrote for the next day's paper. Having followed John Paul to the holy places, having listened to all he said, having spoken to the people who flocked to be with him, I felt it in my bones: These had certainly been days of intense emotion. Consider the scenes in this family photo album: John Paul, looking at the Holy Land from the mount where Moses viewed it at his life's end. John Paul, staring silently into the eternal flame at Yad Vashem, then meeting Holocaust survivors from his hometown. John Paul, achieving his hope of celebrating Mass in Bethlehem. John Paul, exhorting 100,000 young people in sight of the shores where Peter decided to follow Jesus. John Paul, calling on the world to resolve the woes of Palestinian refugees. John Paul, seeking forgiveness at the Western Wall. John Paul, celebrating Mass at the traditional site of the Last Supper. John Paul, praying silently in the Nativity grotto, at Mary's house, at Peter's house, at Gethsemane.

Now, "almost at this journey's end," he wanted to contemplate Mary, who had played a special role for him since his childhood, the journey's beginning. In a visit in 1999 to Wadowice, his hometown, John Paul spoke of how devotion to Our Lady of Mount Carmel "had such a great influence on the spirituality of the Wadowice area." He added, "I myself received many graces there."[23] Devotion to Mary had always been an important part of his life, and now, "touched by the light of the Resurrection," he praised her with titles dear to the Church: *Mater dolorosa*, Mother of Sorrow; *Stella matutina*, Morning star; *Regina in caelum assumpta*, Queen assumed into heaven; *Theotokos*, Mother of God.

But even after this morning of intense emotion—in just a few hours, he had navigated thousands of contentious years in the history of religion—John Paul was not finished. The pope had not gone to Calvary.

As recounted by a church official in Jerusalem, John Paul brought this up with Archbishop Pietro Sambi, the apostolic delegate in Jerusalem. Sambi, who was at John Paul's side throughout the pilgrimage, was returning with the pope to the nuncio's residence on the Mount of Olives after the day's scheduled events were completed.

"You know, I did not get a chance to go to Calvary and would like to do so," the pope said.

Sambi replied, "Your Holiness, it is getting rather late, you have had a full day and besides, the Israeli security and police have gone home."

John Paul grasped Sambi's arm strongly and said, emphatically, "I will not leave this country until I pray at Golgotha."

It must have been an amazing moment. Papal trips are always a security and logistical nightmare, but especially in volatile Jerusalem, with its ancient animosities, unsettled politics and packed, closely confined streets. Every detail was planned, every stop analyzed. Sambi had met time and again with government and religious officials. And now the pope was telling Sambi that he wanted to return to the Old City, which would by then be resuming its usual pace after the morning's rigid security was relaxed. But what could the archbishop do? Out came a cell phone to tell security officials there had been a change of plan. Israeli police quickly told pilgrims to leave the Church of the Holy Sepulchre, and stunned travelers soon saw John Paul return.

The climb to the chapels atop the rock of Calvary would have been difficult for a man in John Paul's physical condition. The stairs, located just to the right of the church's entrance, are steep, narrow and winding. Once he arrived, the Greek Orthodox Church provided a prie-dieu for the pope to kneel, and for 20 minutes, he prayed in silence before the gilded altar marking the place where Jesus was crucified. From his early years, when he became fascinated by Carmelite spirituality and great mystics such as St. John of the Cross, John Paul has been a contemplative. During his closely scrutinized pilgrimage, it seemed he could let the commotion surrounding him fall away in a moment. Now, he wanted to pray alone.

It's no surprise that John Paul so wanted to follow the path to Calvary; for centuries, it has been a magnet for the faithful. Any pilgrim who passed it by would insist on returning, and in this, the pope was very human. But a passage in his writings gives an additional clue to his sense that something very important was missing from his pilgrimage:

"The liturgy of the Eastern Church is fundamentally centered on the Resurrection. The Western Church, while maintaining the primacy of the Resurrection, has gone further in the direction of the Passion. The veneration of Christ's Cross has shaped the history of Christian piety and has inspired the greatest saints. . . . All of them, beginning with Saint Paul, have been 'lovers of the Cross of Christ' (Galatians 6:14). . . . There is no Christian holiness without devotion to the Passion, just as there is no holiness without the centrality of the Paschal Mystery."[24]

In the Catholic tradition, the pope is saying, a balanced spirituality requires a visit to Calvary as well as to the empty tomb. Faith can't focus only on the triumphant, risen Christ. It must also ponder Jesus' humanity, and how God intervenes in the world—which means facing up to the suffering in human beings, in whom God dwells.

This was part of the magic of the papal pilgrimage: John Paul had written throughout his papacy on the importance of the Incarnation, the Crucifixion, the Resurrection. But now his ideas took on flesh as he visited the places where these events occurred.

In his homily at Manger Square in Bethlehem, John Paul closely tied the events that most show Jesus' humanity, his birth and death. His celebration of the Jubilee Year—of God's entry into human history 2,000 years ago—would be incomplete without recognition that the Crib started the path to the Cross. He referred to an early Christian hymn Paul included in his letter to the Philippians, one of the first efforts we know of to make sense of the mystery of the Cross: "Let the same mind be in you that was in Christ Jesus

> who, though he was in the form of God,
> > did not regard equality with God
> > as something to be exploited,
> but emptied himself,
> > taking the form of a slave,
> > being born in human likeness.
> And being found in human form,
> > he humbled himself
> > and became obedient to the point of death—
> > even death on a cross."[25]

As the pope said in Bethlehem, "The great mystery of divine self-emptying, the work of our redemption unfolding in weakness: this is no easy truth." If it was difficult at birth—Jesus, born in poverty—then it was even more so in a degrading, torturous death. If God sent Jesus to show what it means to be fully human, then the Cross is the ultimate example: All must be yielded to God with a self-denying love. Adam failed to understand that as a human being, he was made in God's image. Instead, he grasped at "equality with God." The Cross was the great corrective to Adam's error; it shows how to be truly human, and that to be humble is to be like God.[26]

No, it's not an "easy truth." As John Paul put it in Bethlehem: "The Crib of Jesus lies always in the shadow of the Cross. The silence and poverty of the birth in Bethlehem are one with the darkness and pain of the death on Calvary. The Crib and the Cross are the same mystery of redemptive love; the body which Mary laid in the manger is the same body offered up on the Cross."

Or, as he wrote in his letter *Tertio Millennio*: "The Son of God became man, taking a body and soul in the womb of the Virgin, precisely for this reason: to become the perfect redeeming sacrifice."[27]

Simply put, it was inevitable that this strong-willed pope would insist on visiting the place where Jesus was crucified. He was a pilgrim, as we all are, and the holy places were signposts on his journey toward eternity.

And so we will leave the pilgrim pope here, and perhaps remember him this way, alone before God, on his knees at Calvary. It's possible that on that Sabbath day, that seventh day, he was meditating on the everlasting Eighth Day. We can't know the prayers that were in his heart. Instead, we return to the beginning of Pope John Paul's papacy and the words of his first encyclical:

"The man who wishes to understand himself thoroughly—and not just in accord with immediate, partial, often superficial, and even illusory standards and measures of his being—he must with his unrest, uncertainty and even his weakness and sinfulness, with his life and death, draw near to Christ. He must, so to speak, enter into him with all his own self, he must 'appropriate' and assimilate the whole of the reality of the Incarnation and Redemption in order to find himself. If this profound process takes place within him, he then bears fruit not only of adoration of God but also of deep wonder at himself. How precious must man be in the eyes of the Creator, if he 'gained so great a Redeemer,' and if God 'gave his only Son' in order that man 'should not perish but have eternal life.' "[28]

Questions for Reflection

1. The papal pilgrimage showed once again that religion and politics are a difficult mix in Jerusalem. What do you see as the correct role for religion in civic life? What does Pope John Paul II propose?

2. By admitting Christians' sins from the past, does the pope diminish the Church's credibility today? Do you think he should go further in making such admissions? If so, what should be said about the Holocaust?

3. How do you feel about being asked to share the burden for events that occurred long ago, such as the Crusades and the Inquisition? Can anything really be done at this point?

4. Describe a historical event that has had a strong effect on you.

5. When do you get a sense of the Resurrection, of Christ rising in the world today?

6. Do you share the optimism Pope John Paul II expressed in the Church of the Holy Sepulchre: "Can we doubt that in the power of the Spirit of Life we will be given the strength to overcome our divisions and to work together to build a future of reconciliation, unity and peace?"

7. John Paul wrote that reflecting on the Incarnation and Redemption can give a person a sense of "deep wonder at himself." Given all he said in his speeches and homilies in the Holy Land, can you explain what he means?

8. If you could pick only one place to pray in the Holy Land, which would it be? Why?

Conclusion

SOON after we returned home from the Holy Land, Paul and I received an invitation from Frank DeRosa, the director of public information for the Diocese of Brooklyn, to attend the annual World Communications Day lunch hosted by Bishop Thomas Daily. This event gathers journalists from secular and Catholic newspapers, radio and television stations, to share some conversation and listen to a speaker. On this occasion in early May, it was not one speaker, but a panel of four people who had covered the papal pilgrimage: Bill Bell from the *New York Daily News*, Hugh Mulligan from the Associated Press, Paul and myself.

We had an enjoyable lunch, topped by a stunning dessert: a chocolate replica of the Brooklyn Bridge. Then the four of us sat in front of the other lunch guests and took turns speaking briefly about our experiences covering the pilgrimage. At the end, there was enough time for each of us to make one more comment. Somehow, the microphone came to me last, which gave me the unexpected, unplanned-for opportunity to have the final word. And I felt the need to offer a summary—something a little cosmic.

What I heard myself saying was simply this: Though it is difficult to discern exactly what the Spirit wants to accomplish in a given pontificate, when future historians pass judgment on John Paul, I believe that they will agree on two things. One is that his life experience, surviving the Nazi occupation of Poland and watching so many of his Jewish neighbors sent to the death camps, made him better qualified than any pope in history to bring about a serious reconciliation between Jews and Catholics. On this trip to Israel, he capped his heroic efforts on this issue with his appearance at Yad Vashem, an image that will live forever. The second historical consensus will be that John Paul's work of inspiring and nurturing the Solidarity movement in Poland helped set in motion the forces that led to the fall of communism in Eastern Europe.

Thinking back on it, I can't recall whether I spoke at the lunch about a third area of likely consensus by historians, but let me say it now. Like his biographer, George Weigel, I believe that John Paul has rendered obsolete the stay-in-Rome-and-tend-the-bureaucracy model of papacy. His world travels have established a new norm: the pope as the globe-girdling chief evangelist of the church. Future popes are unlikely to enjoy travel as much as he has, and it is difficult to imagine anyone moving audiences with his combination of intelligence and theatrical talent. But his example will make it very difficult for any future pope to avoid evangelical travels entirely.

At the end of my little cosmic summary, I said something else. Despite his stunning achievements in Jewish-Catholic relations and in geopolitics, John Paul has left some unfinished business. As nearly as I can recall, these were my words: "It will take us another pope or two down the road for women to get their due in our church." At that moment, I thought I heard a few groans, and I wondered later whether I had gone too far. I hadn't exactly planned to say it, and I'm not sure why I did.

Maybe it was a sudden, ungovernable jolt of energy from the chocolate bridge. Maybe it was my inside knowledge, as the husband of Judy, a Catholic school teacher, and the father of Rachel, a student at a Jesuit graduate school. More likely, the immediate stimulus was some grumbling that I had just heard from a group of laywomen who work for the church, not long before I spoke. Beyond that, it may have been the attitudes of some good friends who happen to be nuns—wonderful women who live the Gospel every day in a variety of ministries, from education to caring for people who suffer from AIDS. When John Paul's name comes up in conversation, some of them roll their eyes, frown, or drop caustic little comments. This puts me, the cynical secular journalist, in the odd position of speaking up for John Paul, reminding them of his breathtaking gifts and his earthshaking achievements, even though I agree with them completely on the role of women in the church.

In my own nuanced way, I realize, I really do love this amazing man. As a religion writer for a secular paper, of course, I'm not supposed to have such strong feelings about him. But I was a Catholic long before I first committed journalism, and I expect to be a Catholic until the day they box me and plant me. Besides, when John Paul was elected in 1978, I was still covering politics, not religion, and I was free to say whatever I wanted about him, without violating the unwritten code of journalistic ethics. Soon after that election, as John Paul began to break the mold and travel the world, I remember a non-Catholic colleague saying to me, "Your pope sure knows how to pope." At that moment, I felt immensely proud of John Paul, as I have felt on many occasions since then.

Over the years, though that pride is still strong, it has become mixed with disappointment, as I saw his Curia too often override the authority of bishops, as I learned of the way he once treated Archbishop Oscar Romero, and as I gradually grew to believe that the Vatican had not matched his words about the dignity of women with sufficient action to assure that the Church treats them more equally.

Despite those concerns over women's issues, we can all agree on the value and the lasting significance of his visit to the Holy Land. It is something we should all celebrate. On one of the most heavily reported trips of his pontificate, John Paul's visit to so many places of pilgrimage energized him and gave new shades of meaning to many of his key themes: the dignity of all human beings, the centrality of Jesus, and his own vivid sense of God's presence.

The celebration of John Paul's success on this trip should begin with a recognition that hostility to Judaism has been a consistently dark and ugly stain on Christianity from the beginning. No other pope has been as bold as John Paul in naming the sin and seeking forgiveness. In two moments that can never be forgotten, in the Hall of Remembrance at Yad Vashem and at the Western Wall, the pope put the entire weight of his office into words and images that said simply: We are sorry, and we must never let it happen again.

There are things that John Paul did not accomplish on this pilgrimage. Despite his eloquent calls for peace in the Holy Land, the fighting and killing erupted again only a few months after he left, bringing violence even to Bethlehem and Nazareth, where happy crowds had so recently gathered to cheer him. Nor did his heartfelt desire for Christian unity heal the division between Catholic and Orthodox leaders.

There are also things he accomplished stunningly. One was to encourage and energize the dwindling population of Arab Christians in the Holy Land. Before a crowd of about 100,000 people on the Mount of the Beatitudes, the pope spoke words that could be read as an exhortation to all the Christians of the region to hold fast to their beliefs, even under difficult circumstances. "You hear his voice on this hill, and you believe what he says," John Paul said. "But like the first disciples at the Sea of Galilee, you must leave your boats and nets behind, and that is never easy—especially when you face an uncertain future and are tempted to lose faith in your Christian heritage. To be good Christians may seem beyond your strength in today's world. But Jesus does not stand by and leave you alone to face the challenge."

John Paul's other grand accomplishment was to show himself—in word, image and act—to be a staunch friend of the Jewish people. Among the things I will always remember about this trip are the moments after I had watched his Yad Vashem speech with a group of Holocaust survivors. One of them, David Sealtiel, hidden as a child by a Christian family in Holland, summed up the day and the trip as well as anyone could: "What I hear is what never, ever a pope said before."

—*Bob Keeler*

Suggested Reading

Accattoli, Luigi. *When a Pope Asks Forgiveness: The Mea Culpa's of John Paul II.* Translated by Jordan Aumann, O.P., New York: Alba House, 1998.

Armstrong, Karen. *Jerusalem: One City, Three Faiths.* New York: Knopf, 1996.

Dwyer, John C. *Son of Man & Son of God.* New York: Paulist, 1983. Includes a thought-provoking section on the meaning of the crucifixion.

Eliade, Mircea. *The Sacred and the Profane.* New York: Harcourt, Brace Jovanovich, 1959. Still the best and most concise explanation of the nature of sacred places and times.

Freeman-Grenville, G.S.P., *The Holy Land: A Pilgrim's Guide to Israel, Jordan and the Sinai.* New York: The Continuum Publishing Company, 1996.

Hillesum, Etty. *An Interrupted Life and Letters from Westerbork.* New York: Holt, 1996. One woman's moving, spiritually charged account of the Holocaust.

Idinopulos, Thomas A. *Jerusalem: A History of the Holiest City as Seen Through the Struggles of Jews, Christians, and Muslims.* Chicago: Ivan R. Dee, 1994.

John Paul II. *Crossing the Threshold of Hope.* New York: Knopf, 1994. Includes the pope's thoughts on Islam and Judaism.

John Paul II. *Gift and Mystery: On the Fiftieth Anniversary of My Priestly Ordination.* New York: Doubleday, 1996. The pope reflects on his path to ministry.

Kirsch, Jonathan. *Moses: A Life.* New York: Ballantine Books, 1998.

Murphy-O'Connor, Rev. Jerome. *The Holy Land: An Oxford Archaeological Guide from Earliest Times to 1700.* Oxford: Oxford University Press, 1998. Highly recommended.

Noone, Sister Judith, M.M. *The Same Fate as the Poor.* Maryknoll, New York: Orbis Books, 1995. An excellent account of the murders of the four churchwomen in El Salvador in 1980, which provides food for meditation about the costs of following Jesus, as his disciples first did in Galilee.

O'Brien, Darcy. *The Hidden Pope: The Untold Story of a Lifelong Friendship That is Changing the Relationship Between Catholics and Jews: The Personal Journey of John Paul II and Jerzy Kluger.* New York: Rodale, 1998. An inside look at how John Paul improved Jewish-Catholic relations.

Rolheiser, Ronald. *The Holy Longing: The Search for A Christian Spirituality.* New York: Doubleday, 1999. This excellent book includes sections on spirituality based in the Incarnation and Jesus' death and resurrection.

Rudin, Rabbi A. James. *Israel for Christians: Understanding Modern Israel.* Philadelphia: Fortress Press, 1983.

Wareham, Norman, and Gill, Jill. *Shrines of the Holy Land.* Liguori, Missouri: Liguori, 1998.

Weigel, George. *Witness to Hope: The Biography of Pope John Paul II.* New York: HarperCollins, 1999. The author had unusual access to the pope.

Wilkinson, John. *Egeria's Travels.* London: S.P.C.K., 1971.

Wilkinson, John. *Jerusalem as Jesus Knew It: Archaeology as Evidence.* London: Thames and Hudson, 1978.

Web sites

www.custodia.org/pope, a site maintained by the Franciscan Custody of the Holy Land, memorializes Pope John Paul II's trip, providing the text of all his public statements, brief descriptions and many photos.

www.vatican.va, the official Vatican Web site, offers a searchable on-line library of John Paul's encyclicals, homilies and other writings, including his homilies and speeches in the Holy Land.

End Notes

Introduction

[1] John Paul II, *Redemptor Hominis*, No. 1.

[2] John Paul II, *Tertio Millennio Adveniente*, No. 23.

[3] ibid., No. 1., citing Galatians 4:4.

[4] ibid., No. 14.

[5] Mircea Eliade, *The Sacred and the Profane* (New York: Harcourt, Brace Jovanovich, 1959), p. 88.

[6] *Tertio Millennio Adveniente*, No. 24.

[7] See Eliade, pp. 63-65.

[8] John Paul II, *Letter of the Supreme Pontiff John Paul II Concerning Pilgrimage to the Places Linked to the History of Salvation* (Vatican City: Libreria Editrice Vaticana, June 29, 1999), No. 4, citing Karol Wojtyla, *Poezje. Poems*, Wydawnictwo Literackie, Kraków 1998, p. 168.

[9] ibid., No. 10.

Chapter 1

[1] *Insight Guide Jordan* (London: APA Publications, 1999), p. 139.

[2] ibid., p.142.

[3] Jordanian government web site.

[4] Tareq Ayyoub, "Amman has the lowest hotel occupancy rate in Mideast, study shows," *Jordan Times*, May 20, 1999.

[5] John Paul II, *Letter of the Supreme Pontiff John Paul II Concerning Pilgrimage to the Places Linked to the History of Salvation*, No. 10.

[6] *Insight Guide Jordan*, p. 223.

[7] John 3:14-15.

[8] *Insight Guide Jordan*, p. 223.

[9] "The Pope visits Mount Nebo," web site of the Franciscan Custody of the Holy Land, March 19, 2000. The web site is www.custodia.org.

[10] G.S.P. Freeman-Grenville, *The Holy Land: A Pilgrim's Guide to Israel, Jordan and the Sinai* (New York: The Continuum Publishing Company, 1996), pp. 193-194.

[11] Exodus 3:11.

[12] Exodus 3:14.

[13] Jonathan Kirsch, *Moses: A Life* (New York: Ballantine Books, 1998), pp. 114-116. These pages contain an excellent summary of God's names.

[14] Exodus 4:10.

[15] George Weigel, "Holy Land Pilgrimage: A Diary," *First Things*, June/July 2000, pp. 27-29.

Chapter 2

[1] Genesis 15:8.

[2] Luke 1:18.

[3] Luke 1:63

[4] Raymond E. Brown, *The Birth of the Messiah* (New York: Doubleday, 1993), pp. 350-355.

[5] Luke 1:69-71.

[6] Jeremiah 1:19.

[7] *Merriam Webster's Collegiate Dictionary, Tenth Edition* (Springfield, Massachusetts: Merriam-Webster, 1993).

[8] *Centesimus Annus*, section 42.1 to 42.2.

[9] George Weigel, *Witness to Hope: The Biography of Pope John Paul II* (New York; HarperCollins, 1999), pp. 621-624.

[10] John 1:28.

[11] John 11:1-44.

[12] Joshua 3:1; 2 Kings 2:7-8.

[13] 2 Kings 2:11-14.

[14] "John the Baptist's settlement at 'Bethany beyond the Jordan' sheds new light on baptism tradition in Jordan," by Rami G. Khouri, *Jordan Times*, Amman, Jordan, September 27, 1999.

[15] Daniel J. Harrington, S.J., *Collegeville Bible Commentary: The Gospel According to Matthew* (Collegeville, Minnesota: The Liturgical Press, 1983), p. 21.

[16] Matthew 3:14-15.

[17] Matthew 3:16-17.

Chapter 3

[1] *Tertio Millennio Adveniente*, No. 4.

[2] John Paul II, *Gift and Mystery: On the Fiftieth Anniversary of My Priestly Ordination* (New York: Doubleday, 1996), pp. 66-67.

[3] Weigel, *Witness to Hope*, p. 52.

[4] James Michener, *Poland* (New York: Fawcett Crest, 1983), p. 451, quoted in Weigel, *Witness to Hope*, p. 51.

[5] Weigel, *Witness to Hope*, p. 296.

[6] John Paul II, *Sollicitudo Rei Socialis*, 1987, No. 31.

Chapter 4

[1] Rev. Jerome Murphy-O'Connor, *The Holy Land: An Oxford Archaeological Guide from Earliest Times to 1700* (Oxford: Oxford University Press, 1998), p. 106.

[2] *Merriam Webster's Collegiate Dictionary.*

[3] Philippians 2:7.

[4] © 1973, The Benedictine Foundation of the State of Vermont, Inc.

[5] *Nostra Aetate*, No. 4.

[6] *Gift and Mystery*, p. 36.

[7] ibid., p. 39.

[8] Gian Franco Svidercoschi, *Letter to a Jewish Friend: The Simple and Extraordinary Story of Pope John Paul II and His Jewish School Friend* (New York: The Crossroad Publishing Company, 1994), pp. 93ff.

[9] *Tertio Millennio Adveniente*, No. 53.

[10] Gil Hoffman, *Jerusalem Post*, March 27, 2000.

Chapter 5

[1] 1 Corinthians 1:26.

[2] John 6:68.

[3] Details on the sites in Tabgha and Capernaum came from the Israel Information Center in Jerusalem. More information is available through the Israeli foreign ministry web site: www.mfa.gov.il.

[4] John 21:15-17.

[5] Matthew 9:9.

[6] Matthew 4:13.

[7] Mark 1:22.

[8] Mark 2:3.

[9] Luke 4:34.

[10] John 4:46-53.

[11] Mark 9:35.

[12] John 6:53.

[13] Matthew 8:8; Luke 7:6-7.

[14] Matthew 11:23-24; Luke 10:15.

[15] Encyclical *Ut Unum Sint*, 1995, section 88.

[16] ibid., section 95.

[17] ibid., section 96.

[18] Phyllis Zagano and Terrence W. Tilley, ed., *The Exercise of the Primacy: Continuing the Dialogue* (New York: The Crossroad Publishing Company, 1998), p. 1.

[19] ibid., p. 4.

[20] ibid., p. 11.

[21] *Catholic New York*, July 25, 1996.

Chapter 6

[1] Matthew 2:15.

[2] Matthew 2:16-17.

[3] Matthew 2:23.

[4] Brown, *The Birth of the Messiah*, p. 227.

[5] ibid. pp. 112-113.

[6] Murphy-O'Connor, pp. 375-376; James H. Charlesworth, *The Millennium Guide for Pilgrims to the Holy Land* (New York: D&F Scott Publishing, 2000), pp. 188-190.

[7] Weigel, *Witness to Hope*, p. 440.

[8] "Here I Am, Lord," © 1981, Dan Schutte and New Dawn Music. Based on Isaiah 6.

[9] Judith M. Noone, M.M., *The Same Fate as the Poor* (Maryknoll, New York: Orbis, 1995); Raymond Bonner, *Weakness and Deceit: U.S. Policy and El Salvador* (New York: Times Books, 1984).

[10] Thumbnail biography, Religious Task Force on Central America and Mexico web site, www.rtfcam.org.

[11] Weigel, *Witness to Hope*, p. 456.

[12] Recollections by Giancarlo Zizola, Maria Lopez Vigil and Jon Sobrino in the transcript of the PBS documentary, "John Paul II: The Millennial Pope," available through the PBS web site, www.pbs.org.

[13] Noone, p. 134.

[14] Luke 4:16-21.

[15] Matthew 25:31-46.

[16] Luke 1:52-53.

[17] Brown, *The Birth of the Messiah*, pp. 350-355.

[18] Luke 4:22.

[19] Luke 4:29-30.

[20] Matthew 31:31-32, Mark 4:31-32.

[21] Matthew 20:18.

[22] John 17:21.

[23] Congregation for the Doctrine of the Faith, *Note on the Expression "Sister Churches,"* June 30, 2000, No. 10.

[24] *Dominus Iesus, Declaration on the Unicity and Salvific Universality of Jesus Christ and the Church,* August 6, 2000, No. 17.

Chapter 7

[1] See Thomas A. Idinopulos, *Jerusalem: A History of the Holiest City as Seen Through the Struggles of Jews, Christians, and Muslims* (Chicago, Ivan R. Dee, 1994), p. 227. This book has a very readable history of the Haram al-Sharif. See also Karen Armstrong, *Jerusalem: One City, Three Faiths* (New York: Knopf, 1996), p. 159 and Murphy-O'Connor, pp. 80-96.

[2] *The Anchor Bible Dictionary, Volume VI* (New York: Doubleday, 1992), p. 365. The entry, by Carol Meyers, offers an excellent scholarly overview of the Temple's history.

[3] Luke 1:38.

[4] Luke 1:45.

[5] Luke 2:38.

[6] Luke 2:46.

[7] Luke 19:45-48.

[8] Acts 3:2, 11; 5:12.

[9] Idinopulos, p. 154. See also Luigi Accattoli, *When a Pope Asks Forgiveness: The Mea Culpa's of John Paul II* (New York: Alba House, 1998), p. 85. He notes that Muslim leaders cited the Crusades when they refused to meet with the pope in Nigeria in 1982 and in Kenya in 1995.

[10] Nadav Shragai, "Atop the Temple Mount, Pope stays above the fray," *Ha'aretz*, March 27, 2000.

[11] Psalm 137:5-6.

[12] Armstrong, pp. 329-330.

[13] Luke 2:49.

[14] *The Catholic Encyclopedia, Volume VII* (Robert Appleton Company, 1910). Online Edition, copyright 1999, Kevin Knight.

[15] Hans Küng, *The Church* (New York: Doubleday, Image Books, 1976), p. 185. The book was originally published in 1967.

[16] *Newsweek*, on-line edition, March 11, 2000.

[17] John Paul II, *Incarnationis Mysterium, Bull of Indiction of the Great Jubilee of theYear 2000*, No. 11. Italics added.

[18] *Tertio Millennio Adveniente*, No. 33.

[19] *Incarnationis Mysterium*, No. 11.

[20] See Norman Wareham and Jill Gill, *Shrines of the Holy Land* (Liguori, Mo.: Liguori, 1998), p. 58; Murphy-O'Connor, p. 45.

[21] John Wilkinson, *Egeria's Travels* (London: S.P.C.K., 1971), p. 165.

[22] ibid., pp. 123-124.

[23] *A Pope Remembers: It all Began Here, Address of John Paul II in his native town of Wadowice, June 16, 1999*, cited in *The Pope Speaks*, January-February, 2000, p. 28.

[24] John Paul II, *Crossing the Threshold of Hope* (New York: Knopf, 1994), p. 79.

[25] Philippians 2:5-8.

[26] For an interesting interpretation of the theology of the Cross, see John C. Dwyer, *Son of Man & Son of God* (New York: Paulist, 1983), pp. 155-197.

[27] *Tertio Millennio Adveniente*, No. 7.

[28] *Redemptor Hominis*, No. 10.

Additional Titles Published by Resurrection Press, a Catholic Book Publishing Imprint

A Rachel Rosary Larry Kupferman	$4.50
Blessings All Around Dolores Leckey	$8.95
Catholic Is Wonderful Mitch Finley	$4.95
Come, Celebrate Jesus! Francis X. Gaeta	$4.95
From Holy Hour to Happy Hour Francis X. Gaeta	$7.95
Healing through the Mass Robert DeGrandis, SSJ	$9.95
Our Grounds for Hope Fulton J. Sheen	$7.95
The Healing Rosary Mike D.	$5.95
Healing Your Grief Ruthann Williams, OP	$7.95
Heart Peace Adolfo Quezada	$9.95
Life, Love and Laughter Jim Vlaun	$7.95
Living Each Day by the Power of Faith Barbara Ryan	$8.95
The Joy of Being a Catechist Gloria Durka	$4.95
The Joy of Being a Eucharistic Minister Mitch Finley	$5.95
The Joy of Being a Lector Mitch Finley	$5.95
The Joy of Preaching Rod Damico	$6.95
The Joy of Being an Usher Gretchen Hailer, RSHM	$5.95
Lights in the Darkness Ave Clark, O.P.	$8.95
Loving Yourself for God's Sake Adolfo Quezada	$5.95
Mother Teresa Eugene Palumbo, S.D.B.	$5.95
Practicing the Prayer of Presence van Kaam/Muto	$8.95
5-Minute Miracles Linda Schubert	$4.95
Season of New Beginnings Mitch Finley	$4.95
Season of Promises Mitch Finley	$4.95
Soup Pot Ethel Pochocki	$8.95
Stay with Us John Mullin, SJ	$3.95
Surprising Mary Mitch Finley	$7.95
Teaching as Eucharist Joanmarie Smith	$5.95
What He Did for Love Francis X. Gaeta	$5.95
You Are My Beloved Mitch Finley	$10.95
Your Sacred Story Robert Lauder	$6.95

For a free catalog call 1-800-892-6657